Enhanced Expert Systems

Edited by Petrică Vizureanu

Published in London, United Kingdom

IntechOpen

Supporting open minds since 2005

Enhanced Expert Systems
http://dx.doi.org/10.5772/intechopen.79092
Edited by Petrică Vizureanu

Contributors
Mirko Perkusich, João Nunes, Luiz Antonio Silva, Kyller Gorgônio, Hyggo Almeida, Angelo Perkusich, Igor Sheremet, Marcia Oliveira, Adler Neves, Monica Ferreira Silva Lopes, Amal Saki Malehi, Mina Jahangiri, Petrică Vizureanu

First published in London, United Kingdom, 2019 by IntechOpen
IntechOpen is the global imprint of INTECHOPEN LIMITED, registered in England and Wales, registration number: 11086078, The Shard, 25th floor, 32 London Bridge Street
London, SE19SG – United Kingdom
Printed in Croatia

British Library Cataloguing-in-Publication Data
A catalogue record for this book is available from the British Library

Additional hard and PDF copies can be obtained from orders@intechopen.com

Enhanced Expert Systems
Edited by Petrică Vizureanu
p. cm.
Print ISBN 978-1-83881-885-2
Online ISBN 978-1-83881-886-9
eBook (PDF) ISBN 978-1-83881-887-6

For EU product safety concerns:
IN TECH d.o.o., Prolaz Marije Krucifikse Kozulić 3, 51000 Rijeka, Croatia, info@intechopen.com or visit our website at intechopen.com.

Meet the editor

Petrică Vizureanu was born on October 17, 1967, in Bârlad, Romania. He has an MSc in Heating Equipment (1992) and a PhD (1999), both from "Gh. Asachi" Technical University, Iasi. He has been an assistant (1993–1999), lecturer (1999–2002), and assistant professor (2002–2009) at "Gh. Asachi" Technical University, Iasi, Romania. Currently, he is a professor (2009–) at "Gh. Asachi" Technical University, Iasi, Romania. His research activities include expert systems for heating system programming, computer-assisted design for heating equipment, heating equipment for materials processing, heat transfer, biomaterials, and geopolymers. He has published more than 110 papers in international journals and conferences (proceedings) and 28 books.

Contents

Preface

In developing nonlinear expert system simulation models, the proper selection of input variables is a challenging problem. Therefore, a false combination of input variables could prevent the simulation model from achieving the optimal solution. The presented methodology in this book is an applicable approach to input variable selection in multi-input simulators of expert systems (ES).

Large-scale ES usually have a hierarchical structure, including personnel and various technical devices, which consume various material, financial, and information resources, as well as energy. As a result, they produce new resources (objects), which are delivered to other similar systems. The main features of ES are large dimensionality and high volatility of their structures, equipment, consumed/produced objects, and, above all, operation logics and dynamics. In this way, ES are dedicated to a new knowledge representation model, providing convergence of classical operations research and modern knowledge engineering.

As a theoretical approach, this book develops a primary survey of the knowledge representation model, providing convergence of classical operations research and modern knowledge engineering. This convergence creates new opportunities for complicated problems of formalization and solution by integrating the best features of mathematical programming or constraint programming.

This book is a review of classic and Bayesian classification and regression tree approaches with an emphasis on Bayesian approaches, as a first comprehensive review of Bayesian classification and regression trees. Bayesian trees have advantages in comparison to classic tree-based approaches. But Bayesian tree approaches investigate different tree structures with different splitting variables, splitting rules, and tree sizes, so these models can explore the tree space more than classic tree approaches.

Also presented are three semiautomatic methods, found in an exploratory study through a literature review that reduces the burden for experts. These methods help to minimize the effects of human biases by reducing the parameters that are required to construct complete node probability tables. These methods are highly reliable on the input data elicited from experts and present one of many probability elicitation techniques as an example, which can improve the input data needed by the semiautomatic methods and reduce the garbage in/garbage out effect.

The book presents an online system for a 3D representation of programming students' profiles on software metrics that quantify effort and quality of programming from the analysis of source codes. The advantages of this system are enabling the analysis of where the learning difficulties begin, the monitoring of how a class evolves along a course, and informing assessment criteria through the dynamic composition of rubric representations. The system proposed presents itself as a relevant tool to assist teachers regarding decisions of an evaluative process, assisting students from the beginning to the end of a course.

This book has six chapters and explains that expert systems are products in the field of computer science that attempt to perform as intelligent software. What is remarkable for expert systems is the applicability area and the solving of different issues in many fields or industrial branches.

Petrică Vizureanu
Gheorghe Asachi Technical University of Iași,
Romania

Chapter 1

Introductory Chapter: Enhanced Expert System - A Long-Life Solution

Petrică Vizureanu

1. Introduction

What is the definition of an expert system? An expert system belongs to a field of artificial intelligence, and it is a computer program or a software, which can do the same task of a human expert. It can give reliable advice in a specific area of expertise (its domain)and get new conclusions about difficult activities to examine [1]. An expert system can explain its reasoning everytime and is able to interact with a user in the same way that you might consult a human expert. Also, an expert system can be defined as a software program that can outline reasoned conclusions from an amount of knowledge in a specific domain and aims to develop "smart" programs and applications.

The human experts are not 100% reliable in different domains, which can be taken into consideration the advantages and benefits of all accomplished things, but they may disagree with each other or forget to take into account a crucial parameter before making a decision. A human expert can have unsurpassed knowledge in the field and can gain as much knowledge as possible, but be hopeless explaining that to someone else. Human experts cannot be available all the time; i.e., (i) in a small company, the expert on some area can be ill or on holiday; (ii) your doctor may not be able to see you until next week; and (iii) a human expert can move to another company (taking his expertise with him) or retire.

An expert system does not get tired. An expert system (properly programmed) should be 100% reliable and can combine the expertise of several experts. An expert system should be realized to explain and justify all advices it gives. Although an expert system can be expensive to develop, once it is there, its running costs should be low, so there will be economic benefits for the company. An expert system is always available. You can take it with you if you have a notebook or Internet connection, so you could consult an expert system over the Internet. Once the knowledge has been programmed/inserted into the system, it will not be lost if the human expert leaves or dies [2].

Problems with expert systems: limited domain; systems are not always up to date and do not learn, has no "common sense" and experts are needed to setup and maintain the system.

Many applications of expert systems are very well known: Prospector—used by geologists to identify sites for drilling or mining; PUFF—medical system for diagnosis of respiratory conditions; Design Advisor—gives advice to designers of processor chips; MYCIN—medical system for diagnosing blood disorders (first used in 1979); LITHIAN—gives advice to archeologists examining stone tools; and DENDRAL—used to identify the structure of chemical compounds (first used in 1965).

IntechOpen

Main components of an expert system: (i) the knowledge base is the collection of facts and rules which describe all the knowledge about the problem domain; (ii) the inference engine is the part of the system that chooses which facts and rules to apply when trying to solve the user's query; and (iii) the user interface is the part of the system that takes in the user's query in a readable form and passes it to the inference engine. It then displays the results to the user [3].

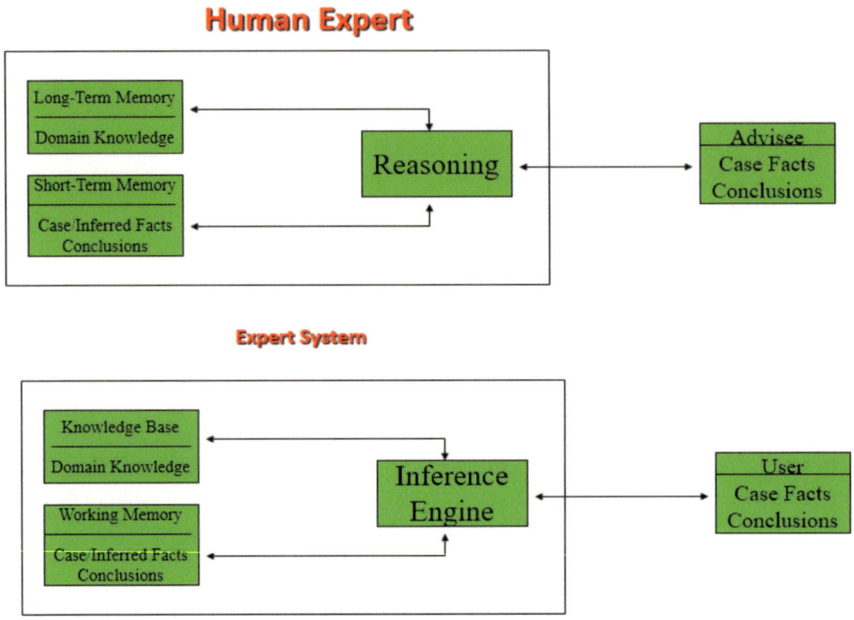

Figure 1.
General description for human expert vs. expert system.

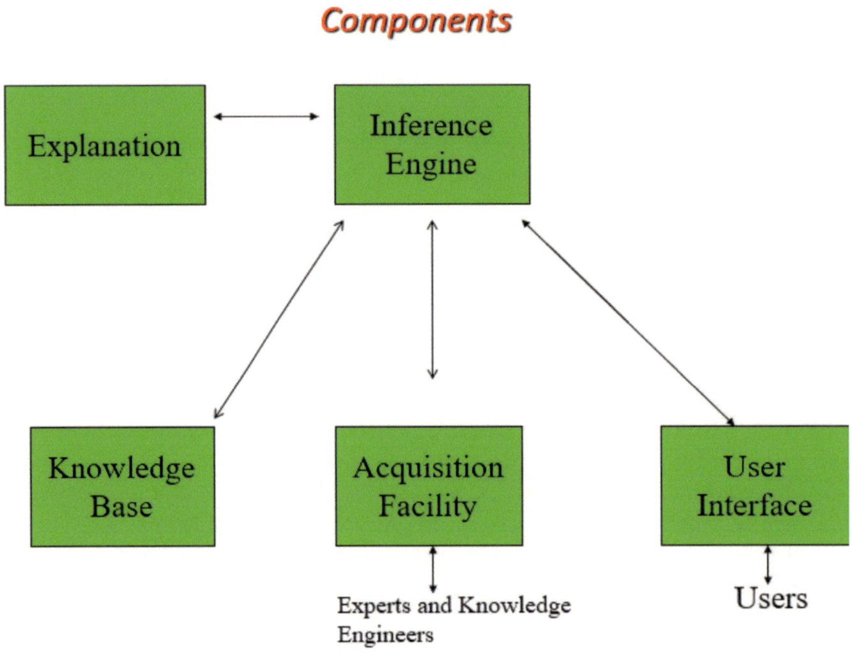

Figure 2.
Main elements of an expert system.

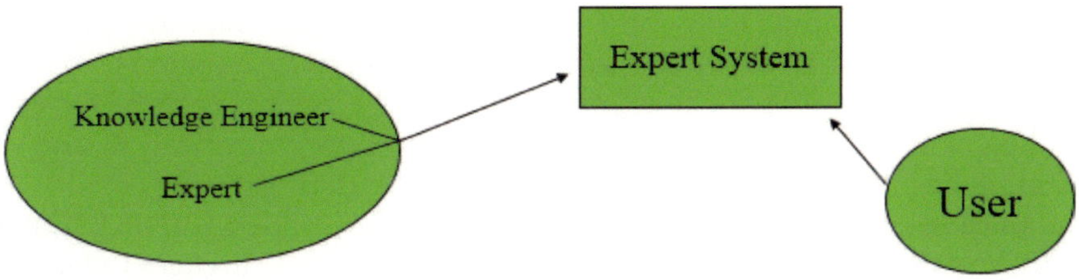

Figure 3.
Logical flow inside an expert system.

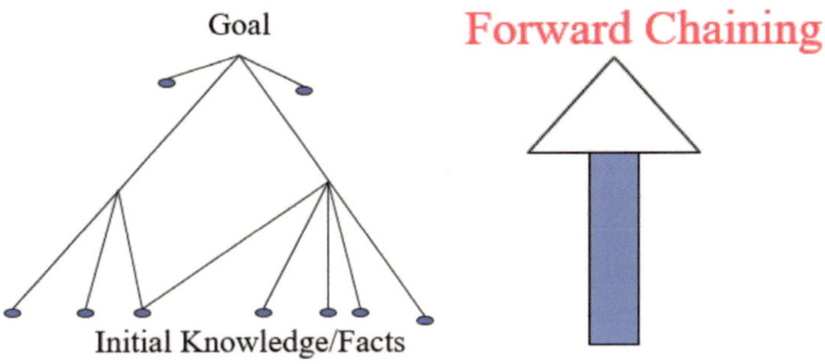

Figure 4.
Forward-chaining technique for an expert system.

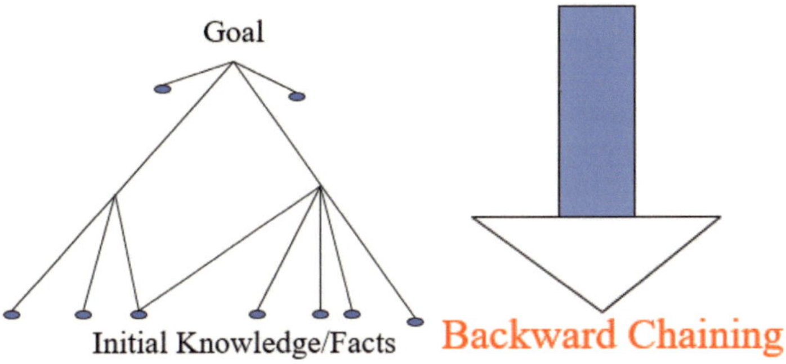

Figure 5.
Backward-chaining technique for an expert system.

An expert system behaves similar to a human expert in a field or area. Also, they can be used to solve problems in various fields or disciplines, and can assist in problem solving, but the goal is not to replace the experts, but to provide users an effective tool thereby relieving experts of routine tasks.

An expert system has some capabilities: (i) superior problem solving—only solvable problems, (ii) ability to save and apply knowledge and experience to problems, (iii) reduced time for complex problems, and (iv) looks at problems from a variety of perspectives.

An expert system has five *basic components:* knowledge base, inference engine, explanation component, user interface, and acquisition component.

Knowledge base contains the factual and empirical knowledge of experts in a particular subject area and all the facts, rules and procedures, which are important for problem solving.

Inference engine simulates the problem-solving strategy of a human expert, represents the logical unit by means of which conclusions are drawn from the knowledge base according to a defined problem-solving method, controls the execution, which questions to ask and in what order, and simulates the problem-solving process of human experts. Functions of the inference engine are to determine which actions are to be executed between individual parts of the expert system, how they are executed, and in what sequence, to determine how and when the rules will be processed and to control the dialog with the user [4].

Explanation component has the role to explain the problem-solving strategy to the user. The solutions must be reproducible by the user and engineer but can only be verified by the human expert: which facts were asked for? why? which facts were vital? and can go as far as, how would the conclusion change if some facts would change?

User interface employs natural language for dialogs with the user whenever possible. Questions posed such as "how should questions be answered by the user?", "how will system responses to these questions will be formulated?", and "what info is to be graphical?" must be easy to use, erroneous errors kept to a minimum, and questions and answers must be understandable.

Acquisition component provides support for structuring and implementation of the knowledge in the knowledge base; hence, it is very important because it allows the engineer to concentrate less on the programming. Knowledge data should be easy to enter, easy to understand methods of representing all info in knowledge base, syntax checks, and access to programming language.

People involved with expert systems are **domain expert** (a person who possesses the skill and knowledge to solve a specific problem in a manner superior to others), **knowledge engineer** (a person who designs, builds, and tests an expert system), and **end-user** (an individual or group who will be using the expert system).

Two main inference techniques are used: forward chaining and backward chaining.

Forward chaining is about the knowledge base searched for rules that match the known facts, and the action part of these rules is performed. The process continues until a goal is reached and puts the symptoms together to reach a conclusion that an ex. doctor has diagnosed in a patient.

Backward chaining starts from a goal, the conclusion. All the rules that contain this conclusion are then checked to determine whether the conditions of these rules have been satisfied. Ex. doctor has an end idea of what is wrong with the patient, though they must prove it by going from the diagnosis and finding the symptoms.

Expert systems have applications, in example, for automatic mapping profiles in software metrics for temporal analysis of programming learning and scoring rubrics. Also, these can be dedicated to a new knowledge representation model, providing convergence of classical operations research and modern knowledge engineering or to a mathematical model that graphically and numerically represents the probabilistic relationships between random variables.

Author details

Petrică Vizureanu
Technical University of Iasi, Romania

*Address all correspondence to: peviz2002@yahoo.com

References

[1] https://torry.aberdeen.sch.uk

[2] http://www.duncanrig.s-lanark.sch.uk

[3] http://www.test-me.co.uk

[4] Kalogirou SA. Artificial intelligence for the modeling and control of combustion processes: A review. Progress in Energy and Combustion Science. 2003;**29**(6):515-566

Chapter 2

Issues in the Probability Elicitation Process of Expert-Based Bayesian Networks

João Nunes, Mirko Barbosa, Luiz Silva, Kyller Gorgônio, Hyggo Almeida and Angelo Perkusich

Abstract

A major challenge in constructing a Bayesian network (BN) is defining the node probability tables (NPT), which can be learned from data or elicited from domain experts. In practice, it is common not to have enough data for learning, and elicitation from experts is the only option. However, the complexity of defining NPT grows exponentially, making their elicitation process costly and error-prone. In this research, we conducted an exploratory study through a literature review that identified the main issues related to the task of probability elicitation and solutions to construct large-scale NPT while reducing the exposure to these issues. In this chapter, we present in detail three semiautomatic methods that reduce the burden for experts. We discuss the benefits and drawbacks of these methods, and present directions on how to improve them.

Keywords: Bayesian networks, probability elicitation, node probability table, expert systems, artificial intelligence

1. Introduction

Bayesian network (BN) is a mathematical model that graphically and numerically represents the probabilistic relationships between random variables through the Bayes theorem. This technique is becoming popular to aid in decision-making in several domains due to the evolution of the computational capacity that makes possible the calculation of complex BN [1]. Some examples of BN application areas are: software development project management [2, 3]; large-scale engineering projects [4]; and the prediction of success in innovation projects [5].

On the other hand, there are open challenges related to the construction of BN. One of these challenges is to build the node probability tables (NPT). In cases where there are databases with enough information for the problem in question, it is possible to automate the process of constructing NPT through *batch learning* [6]. Unfortunately, in practice, in most cases, there is not enough data. That is, it is necessary to collect expert data and manually define the NPT [1].

Furthermore, experts can often understand and identify key relationships that data alone may fail to discover [7]. Therefore, the concept of smart data is defined by [7]: a method that supports data engineering and knowledge engineering approaches with emphasis on applying causal knowledge and real-world facts to develop models.

In this context, it is necessary to manually elicit data from experts to define the NPT. However, given that the complexity of defining NPT increases exponentially, for large-scale BN, it becomes impracticable to manually define all the probability functions that compose each NPT [1]. In addition, experts often have time constraints and are rarely interested in manually defining NPT, partially because it is necessary to work with many probabilistic distributions for long periods [8].

In addition, other factors may compromise the process of probability elicitation to construct the NPT, such as commonly used heuristics. Some well know heuristics used to reduce the cognitive effort in probability assessment task may lead the expert towards biased judgment of probability, leading to systematic errors. Moreover, the experts are hardly able to keep mutually consistent distributions during the NPT definition [1]. In addition, factors such as boredom and fatigue are enough to make the criteria deviate during probability assessment [8], when in fact, it should be uniformly applied throughout the whole elicitation process.

A solution to solve this problem has been proposed by [1], which will be referenced herein as the ranked nodes method (RNM). Its goal is to define the NPT of the parent nodes and then generate the NPT of the child nodes. Ref. [1] introduces the concept of ranked nodes, ordinal random variables represented on a monotonically ordered continuous scale. A fundamental feature of this method is that mathematical expressions generate the child node's NPT. These expressions define the central tendency of the child node for each combination of states of the parent nodes and have as input a set of weights of the parent nodes, which quantifies the relative strengths of their influence on the child node, and a variance parameter.

Another approach was proposed by [8], which will be referenced here as the weighted sum algorithm (WSA). This method uses well know heuristics in its favor, more precisely, the availability [9] heuristic and the simulation [10] heuristic. The main focus of this method is to assemble part of the NPT from experts by asking questions that comprehend cases that are easy to recall by experts, which is likely to be associated to more realistic probabilities. In the WSA, the remainder of the NPT is generated using interpolation techniques.

A systematic approach to generate NPT of nodes with multiple parents is proposed in [11]. This approach is an adaptation of the analytic hierarchy process (AHP) method for the task of probability elicitation and semiautomatic generation of NPT, in which the expert needs only to make the assessment of probabilities conditioned on single parents. In this approach, the probability assessment is indirect by means of paired state judgments and the NPT is generated through the calculation of the product of the probabilities of the child node conditioned on single parents.

The three methods stated above reduce the burden for experts and allow the construction of complex BN in which manual elicitation of the NPT is unfeasible and, generally, there is not enough data to use batch learning. The reduced number of parameters to generate the NPT and consequently, reduced number of questions to ask the experts, makes it easier for the facilitator (e.g., BN expert) to deal with heuristics and possible biases during the NPT construction process. These methods can yet be extended with elaborate probability elicitation techniques (i.e., to improve its input).

Therefore, the objective of this research is to assess in detail three semiautomatic methods to generate NPT. We identified these methods in an exploratory study through a literature review. Additionally, we present heuristics that must be acknowledged during probability assessment for NPT construction and discuss extensions to these methods. It is our understanding that these methods can yet benefit from elaborate probability elicitation techniques. Such techniques can add additional overhead when manually defining the NPT, but this overhead is hugely reduced with semiautomatic methods (i.e., given the reduced number of questions to ask the experts) making them a viable choice to improve the method's input.

This chapter is organized as follows. Section 2 presents an introduction to BN. Section 3 presents common heuristics which should be acknowledged and considered during the probability elicitation process. Section 4 presents a probability elicitation technique which can extend some of the semiautomatic methods. Section 5 presents three semiautomatic methods to generate NPT. Section 6 presents our conclusions and future works.

2. Background

Bayesian networks are graph models used to represent knowledge about an uncertain domain [12]. The Bayesian network, B, is a directed acyclic graph that represents a joint probability distribution over a set of random variables V [13]. The network is defined by the pair $B = \{G, \theta\}$, where $G = (V, E)$ is a directed acyclic graph with nodes V representing random variables and edges E representing the direct dependencies between these variables. θ is the set of probability functions (i.e., node probability table) which contains the parameter $\theta_{v_i}|\pi_i = P_B(v_i|\pi_i)$ for each v_i in V_i conditioned by π_i, the set of parameters of V_i in G. Eq. (1) portraits the joint probability distribution defined by B over V. An example of a BN is depicted in **Figure 1**.

$$P_B(V_1, \ldots, V_n) = \prod_{i=1}^{n} P_B(V_i|\pi_i) = \prod_{i=1}^{n} \theta_{V_i}|\pi_i \tag{1}$$

In the above example, the probability of a person having cancer is calculated according to two variables: "Relatives had cancer" (Y_1) and "Smoke" (Y_2). The ellipses represent the nodes and the arrows represent the arcs. Even though the arcs represent the causal connection's direction between the variables, information can propagate in any direction [14]. Hence, the direction of the arrows indicates the dependency to define the probability functions. In this example, it is assumed that all the variables are Booleans. Since the node "Cancer" is pointed out by Y_1 and Y_2, the probability function is composed of probabilities for all possible combinations of states of Y_1 and Y_2.

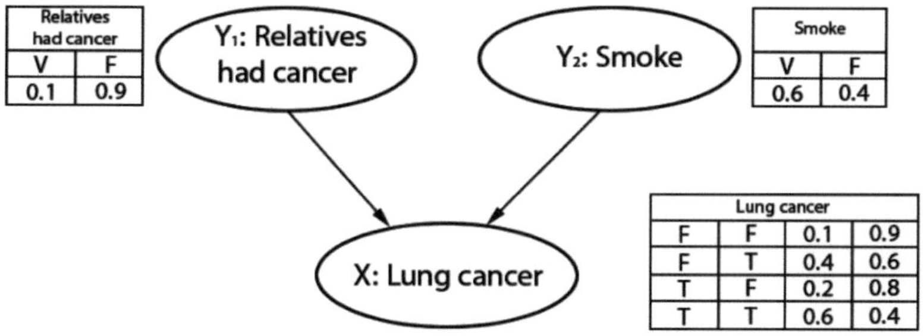

Figure 1.
BN example.

2.1 NPT's complexity

A challenge in constructing a BN is defining the NPT, which can be learned from data or elicited from domain experts. In practice, it is common not to have enough data for learning and elicitation from experts is the only option. However, the complexity of defining NPT grows exponentially, which makes the elicitation process costly and error-prone.

Let us consider the following example shown in **Figure 2**. In this BN, we want to assess *Teamwork* efficiency of a group of people that works collectively to achieve certain goals. *Teamwork* is directly influenced by *Autonomy* (i.e., self-management ability and shared leadership); *Cohesion* (i.e., the capacity of being in close agreement and work well together); and *Collaboration* (i.e., the ability to communicate and coordinate). This example will be used throughout this chapter.

To elicit all the probabilities needed to construct the NPT of the child node *Teamwork*, a facilitator (e.g., BN expert) has to ask 5^3 questions to the expert, a question for each $P(v_i|\pi_i)$. As we can see, the complexity of performing this task grows exponentially as the number of parents increases, making it quite expensive and error-prone.

Methods to address this problem were proposed. Noisy-OR and Noisy-MAX are two popular ones. However, the disadvantage of Noisy-OR is that it only applies to Boolean nodes. According to [1], the disadvantage of Noisy-MAX is that it does not model the extent of relationships required for large-scale BN. In this chapter, we present methods found in the literature that are applicable to a larger range of BN.

3. Heuristics in probability

The quantification process of a BN consists in converting expert knowledge, acquired through personal experiences, into probabilistic knowledge by eliciting a large number of subjective probabilities that reflect the expert's belief at a given moment about something. Probability assessment can be described as the task of quantifying the chances of an event occur, using percentages. However, as the degree of complexity increases, it becomes increasingly difficult to size the probability of occurrence of each of the possible events in a given scenario.

For instance, we may have a hunch as to who will be the winner of a particular tournament at a particular time, but we will never know for sure the exact probability since the number of factors that can influence the event goes beyond our reach. Apart from that, epistemic uncertainties (e.g., lack of knowledge about all

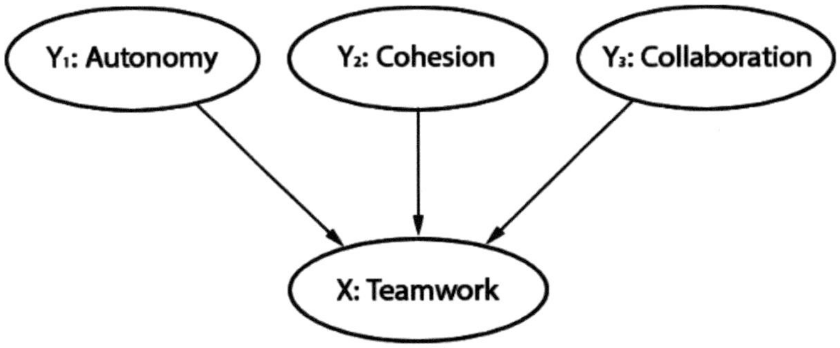

Figure 2.
BN example adapted from [15] where a child node Teamwork *is influenced by three parent nodes:* Autonomy *(Y_1),* Cohesion *(Y_2), and* Collaboration *(Y_3). Each node has five ordinal states: very low (VL), low (L), median (M), high (H), very high (VH).*

the participants in the tournament) and aleatory uncertainties (e.g., possibility of a team losing a player) play an important role in probability assessment. Nonetheless, if asked, one is capable of making an evaluation and give a quick answer. How do people manage to judge the probability of highly uncertain events?

According to [16], people make use of a limited number of heuristics, mental shortcuts, to reduce the complexity of judging the probability of an uncertain event. These mental shortcuts reduce the cognitive effort required to judge the probability of such events. However, they can lead to biases that result in systematic errors. In [16], three commonly used heuristics are presented: representativeness; availability; and anchoring.

The representative heuristic [16] describes the process by which people use the similarity of two events to estimate the degree to which one event is representative of another. It is used to answer questions such as: What is the probability that an event A originates from a process B? What is the probability of a process B generating event A? That is, if A is highly representative of B, the probability of A generating B is considered high. Conversely, if A is not representative of B, the probability of A originating from B is low.

Consider the following example adapted from [16]: *"Steve is very shy and withdrawn, has little interest in people, or in the real world. He has need for order and organization, and a passion for details"*. Based on this description, what is Steven's most likely profession? Farmer or Librarian? You probably thought of a librarian. That happens because the probability of Steve's profession be a librarian is evaluated by the degree to which he is representative, or similar to, the stereotype of a librarian. However, several other factors that should have a significant effect on probability, like the prior probability, or base-rate frequency of the outcomes have no effect on representativeness. For example, the fact that there are many more farmers than librarians should be considered in this case, but it is neglected.

The availability heuristic [9, 16] is related to the judgment of probability of events occurring based on the ease with which we retrieve instances of these events in our mind. For example, to evaluate the likelihood that a person under the age of 30 years will suffer a heart attack, people usually do a quick search in their memory for cases they know of young people who have suffered a heart attack. This heuristic is useful because instances of larger classes are easier to remember than instances of smaller classes. However, the availability is affected by factors other than the frequency of events or probability. One may overestimate the probability of a young person getting cancer based on how recent an instance of such an event has occurred in his life, for example.

Anchoring and adjustment heuristic [16] occur when people judge probabilities based on an initial value, which is adjusted until the final response is reached. The problem with this heuristic is that the adjustments are usually insufficient. In other words, the expert assessment is likely to fluctuate around the initial anchor provided. It is important noting that, an anchor may be embedded in the formulation of a question to the domain expert (i.e., when a starting point is given), but it can also be the result of an incomplete computation.

In short, heuristics are mental shortcuts that reduce the cognitive effort in the task of reasoning about the probability of events with uncertainty. Although useful, it has its disadvantages that must be considered in the knowledge elicitation process. Therefore, it is imperative to acknowledge the possible biases derived from heuristics during the process of probability assessment, explicitly informing the experts of their existence and adopting appropriate methods to reduce their effects.

The number of probabilities to be elicited to construct an NPT may inevitably fall under some bias considering the effort needed from the experts. The semiautomatic methods reduce the number of questions to be asked to the expert or entirely removes the need of direct evaluation of probabilities during the construction of the NPT, which makes it easier for the facilitator and the expert to deal with these heuristics during the elicitation process, seizing the benefits of the heuristics and reducing their possible negative effects.

4. Probability elicitation methods

The process of probability elicitation can be supported by a variety of techniques designed to aid experts when they find it hard to express their degrees of belief with numbers. These methods are based on setting-controlled situations in which probability assessments can be inferred from the expert's behaviors [17]. In this section, we describe the use of probability scales with visual aids to make probability assessment easier for experts. However, it is worth noting, visual aids like probability scales (i.e., which uses numbers) still tend to be biased.

It is our understanding that the use of visual elements such as probability scales can improve the input quality of semiautomatic methods (i.e., the ones which needs probability distributions as input), but indirect methods, which we do not discuss here, may improve the input quality as well. Several methods for indirect elicitation of probabilities have been developed. Some well know methods are: the odds method; the bid method; the lottery method; the probability-wheel method; among others [17, 18], these methods allow the extraction of probabilities without have to explicitly mention probabilities, so to speak.

Both direct and indirect methods can be incorporated at some degree into semiautomatic methods. The purpose of this section is to show one of these techniques which can extend semiautomatic methods, as an example. Also, different techniques may produce different results, so we encourage readers to check a comprehensive review of issues related to the probability elicitation task which has a section dedicated for direct and indirect methods [17].

4.1 Probability scale

A probability scale is composed of a line that can be arranged vertically or horizontally with discrete numerical anchors which denotes the probabilities. It is a direct probability assessment method. To assess a probability, the experts mark a position on the scale. The probability value is given by the marking distance to the zero point of the scale. An example of a numerical probability scale can be seen in **Figure 3**.

There is no standard scale. For instance, anchors may vary in distance and values according to the domain, and lines can be arranged in different positions. Moreover, during probability assessment, one can use both numerical and verbal anchors. In [19] it is proposed a double scale that combines numbers and textual descriptions of probability to aid in the communication of probabilities. According to [19], verbal descriptions commonly used by people to express probabilities are directly related to the numerical values of the probabilities itself. In **Figure 4**, we can see an example of a double scale arranged in the vertical position with numerical and verbal anchors.

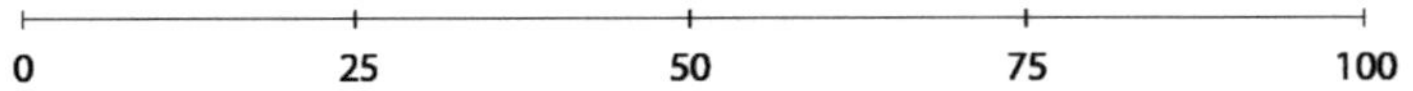

Figure 3.
Probability scale with numerical anchors.

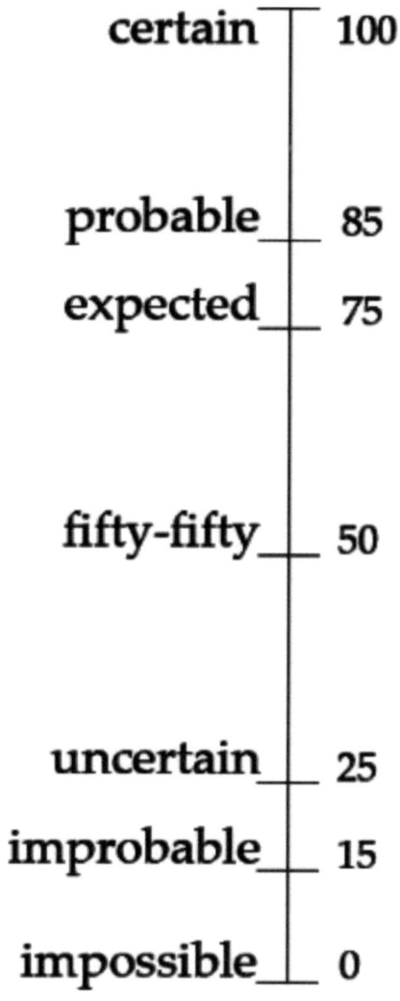

Figure 4.
Probability scale with numbers and words.

The advantage of using a scale is that it allows for the domain experts to think in terms of visual proportion rather than in terms of precise numbers. However, it is important to consider bias that may be introduced using probability scales. For example, let us say an expert is requested to indicate several assessments on a single line. In such a case, he is likely to introduce bias towards esthetically distributed marks. This bias is known as the spacing effect [17] and can be easily avoided by using a separate scale for each probability. Another bias that may be introduced by the use of probability scales is the tendency of people to use the middle of the scale. This bias is known as the centering effect [17].

Furthermore, scales can be used in combination with other components that may help in the task of probability assessment. In [20], a method is presented for elicitation of a large number of conditional probabilities in short time. This method was used to build a real-world BN for the diagnosis of esophageal cancer with more than 4000 conditional probabilities. This BN predicted the correct cancer stage for 85% of the patients [21]. The main idea of this method is to present to the expert a figure with a double scale and a text fragment for each conditional probability. An example of combining probability scales with other components can be seen in **Figure 5**.

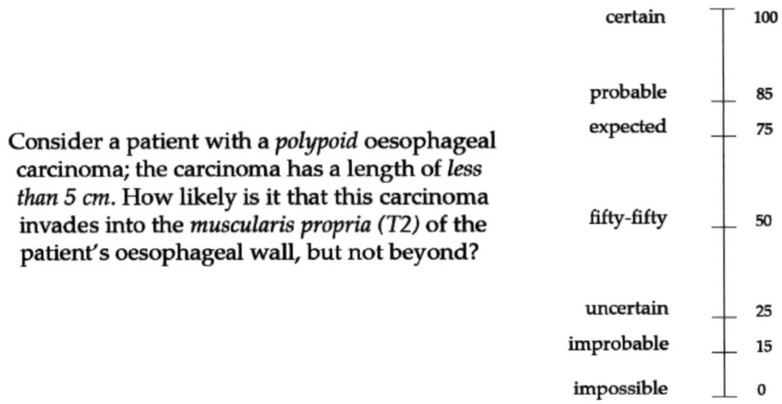

Figure 5.
Text fragment combined with a double scale for probability assessment.

On the left side is a text fragment describing the conditional probability to be assessed. On the right side, we have the double scale proposed in [19]. The text fragment is stated in terms of likelihood rather than frequency which circumvents the need for mathematical notation of the conditional probability. According to [21], the frequency format has been reported to be less liable to lead to biases and experts may experience considerable difficulty understanding conditional probabilities in mathematical notation. Conversely, such an approach may be less intuitive for domains in which it is difficult to imagine 100 occurrences of a rare event.

Nonetheless, in [20], the fragments of text and associated scales are grouped up accordingly to the conditional probability distribution. In so doing, domain experts can assess probabilities from the same conditional probability distribution simultaneously. In other words, the centering effect is avoided by presenting all the related probabilities (i.e., from the same probability distribution) at once for the expert to assess. This approach considerable reduces the number of mental changes during the probability elicitation process. In regards to the spacing effect, the proposed method avoids it by using a separated scale for each probability.

5. Semiautomatic methods

In this section, we present three methods to generate NPT that ease the burden for experts during the quantification process of a BN. These methods allow the construction of large-scale BN. The first is the RNM, which completely eliminates the need for direct probability assessment. The second is the WSA, which is based on two heuristics and needs only part of the NPT to be elicited from the expert. The third is an adaptation of the analytic hierarchy process (AHP) which reduces the cognitive effort, biases and inaccuracies from estimating probabilities to all combinations of states of multiple parents at a time. From now on, we will reference the latter as simply AHP. These three methods attack the magnitude problem of building NPT.

5.1 RNM

In [1], the ranked nodes method (RNM) is presented. In this chapter, it is introduced the concept of ranked nodes, ordinal random variables represented on a

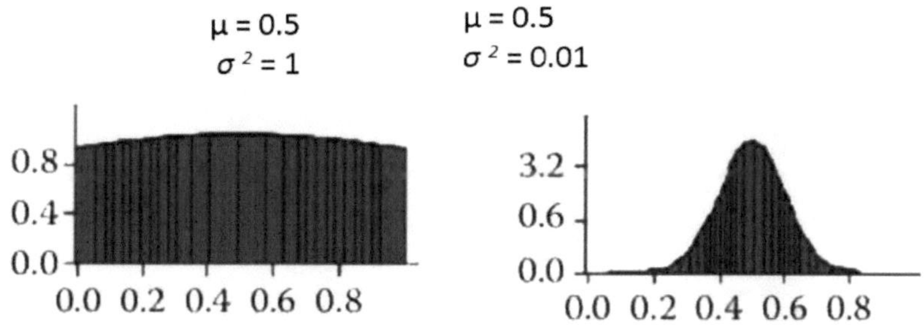

Figure 6.
Examples of TNormal.

continuous scale ordered monotonically in the interval [0, 1]. For example, for the ordinal scale ["Low", "Medium", "High"], "Low" is represented by the interval [0, 1/3], "Medium", by the interval [1/3, 2/3], and "High", by the interval [2/3, 1]. This concept is based on the doubly truncated Normal (TNormal) distribution.

A normal distribution is made of four parameters: μ, mean (i.e., central tendency); σ^2, variance (i.e., uncertainty about the central tendency); a, the lower bound (i.e., 0); and, b, upper bound (i.e., 1). With a normal distribution, it is possible to model a variety of curves (i.e., relationships) as a uniform distribution, achieved when $\sigma^2 = \infty$, and highly skewed distributions, achieved when $\sigma^2 = 0$. In **Figure 6**, we show an example of TNormal with same μ but different σ^2.

In this method, μ is defined by a weighted function of the parent nodes. There are four function types: weighted mean (*WMEAN*) Eq. (2), weighted minimum (*WMIN*) Eq. (3), weighted maximum (*WMAX*) Eq. (4) and a mix of both MIN and MAX functions (*MIXMINMAX*) Eq. (5). In practice, these functions define the central tendency of the child node for the combination of parent nodes states. The weight of each parent node, which quantifies the relative strengths of the influences of the parents on the child node, must be defined by a constant w in which $w \in \mathbb{N}$.

$$WMEAN(z_1, k, \ldots, z_n, k, w_1, \ldots, w_n) = \frac{\sum_{i=1}^{n} w_i * z_i, k}{\sum_{i=1}^{n} w_i} \tag{2}$$

$$WMIN(z_1, k, \ldots, z_n, k, w_1, \ldots, w_n) = \min_{i=1,\ldots,n} \left\{ \frac{w_i * z_i, k + \sum_{j \neq 1}^{n} z_j, k}{w_i + n - 1} \right\} \tag{3}$$

$$WMAX(z_1, k, \ldots, z_n, k, w_1, \ldots, w_n) = \max_{i=1,\ldots,n} \left\{ \frac{w_i * z_i, k + \sum_{j \neq 1}^{n} z_j, k}{w_i + n - 1} \right\} \tag{4}$$

$$MIXMINMAX(z_1, k, \ldots, z_n, k, wmin, wmax) = \frac{WMIN * \min_{i=1,\ldots,n}\{z_i, k\} + WMAX * \max_{i=1,\ldots,n}\{z_i, k\}}{WMIN + WMAX} \tag{5}$$

Fenton et al. [1] do not present the details to, in practice, implement the solution. Despite presenting the mixture functions, there is no information regarding the algorithms used to generate and mix TNormal, define samples size and define a conventional NPT given the calculated TNormals. The latter enables the integration of ranked nodes with other types of nodes such as Boolean and continuous, which brings more modeling flexibility.

In [22], it is proposed a probabilistic algorithm for this purpose, composed of two main steps: (i) generate samples for the parent nodes and

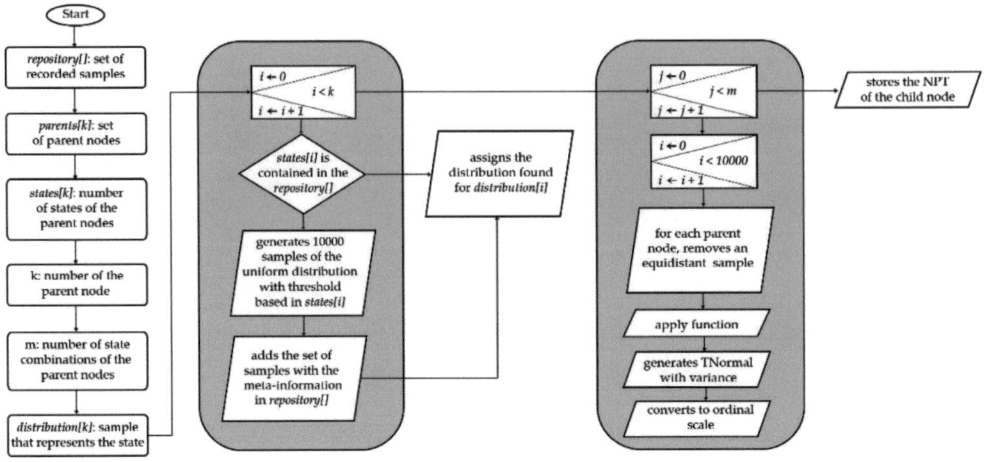

Figure 7.
Overview of the algorithm.

(ii) construct the NPT. In step (ii), for each possible combination of values for the parent nodes (i.e., each column of the NPT), the samples defined in the previous step are mixed given a function selected by the user and a TNormal is generated using the resulting mix and a variance defined by the user. An overview of the algorithm is shown in **Figure 7**.

As already mentioned, a ranked node is conceptually represented by an ordinal scale, which is mapped to the continuous interval [0, 1]. Thus, it is represented as a set of uniform distributions. For an ordinal scale with three values (e.g., “Bad”, “Moderate” and “Good”): $U(0,1) = pbad * U(0,1/3) \cup pmoderate * U(1/3,2/3) \cup pgood * U(2/3,1)$, where p is the density of the distribution.

For the example shown in **Figure 8**, the set of uniform distributions is composed of the union of three uniform distributions: $U(0,1) = 54.7 * U(0,1/3) \cup 36.5 * U(1/3,2/3) \cup 8.80 * U(2/3,1)$. Numerically, this union is calculated using samples. Considering a sample size of 10,000, to represent the NPT of the example shown in **Figure 8**, it is necessary to collect 5700 random samples from $U(0,1/3)$, 3650 random samples from $U(1/3,2/3)$ and 880 random samples from $U(2/3,1)$.

Figure 7 shows that the algorithm is composed of four collections: $repository[]$, a vector to store the samples of base states for the parent nodes; $parents[k]$, a vector to store references to the parent nodes of each child node, in which k is the number of parents; $states[m]$, a vector to store the states of each node, in which m is the number of possible values for the child node given the combination states of its parents; and $distribution[m]$, a vector to store the resulting distribution for each possible combination of states of the parent nodes.

The repository strategy is used for optimization purposes. First, it is registered in memory (i.e., in $repository[]$) distributions that represent the base states, which are states with hard evidence (i.e., a node has 100% of chance for a given state). For instance, for a node composed of the states [“Bad”, “Moderate”, “Good”], are registered samples for: 100% “Bad”, 100% “Moderate” and 100% “Good”, which respectively has $\mu = 1/6$, $\mu = 1/2$ and $\mu = 5/6$. For this purpose, samples from a uniform distribution with the limits defined given the thresholds of the scale are collected.

For instance, for 100% “Good”, it is collected samples of a uniform distribution limited in the interval [2/3, 1]. In [22] it is empirically defined that using a sample size of 10,000 is enough to guarantee a margin of error less than 0.1%. Each sample

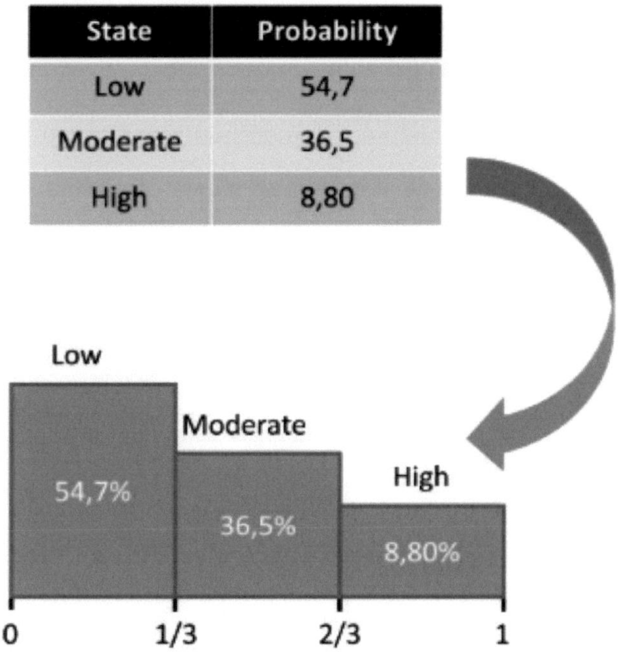

Figure 8.
Conversion from ordinal to continuous scale.

is registered with meta-data regarding its configuration (i.e., number of states and μ). The data in *repository*[] is used to generate samples for a node. Therefore, the samples for a base state are only generated once and reused later. The next step consists of, for each combination of the parent nodes, mix the TNormal using equidistant samples, randomly selected for each parent node. The samples are mixed using one of the given functions (e.g., *WMEAN*, *WMIN*, *WMAX* or *MIXMINMAX*) and the defined variance.

To mix the distributions, a random element from each sample of the parents is removed and used to calculate a resulting element using a given function. For instance, consider node A with two parents B and C. If we are calculating the probabilities of A for the combination "Low"-"High" and the selected function is *WMEAN* with equal weights, if the values removed in an iteration were 0.1 and 0.7, the resulting value would be 0.4. This step must be repeated until the collections of samples are empty.

Afterwards, the set of calculated elements and the given σ are used as input to generate a TNormal. The resulting distribution is converted to an ordinal scale and represents a column in the NPT of the child node (i.e., in the given example, the column for the combination "Low"-"High"). At the end of this step, all the possible combinations of states of the parent nodes are evaluated and the NPT for the child node is completed.

Accordingly, the inputs to generate the NPT of a child node are: a weighted expression capable of generating curves equivalent to distributions expected by the experts; a set of weights of the parent nodes; and a value for σ^2. To determine the weighted expression one can ask the experts to assess the mode of the child node for different combinations of the extreme states of the parent nodes [23]. For instance, let us consider the Bayesian network shown in **Figure 8** along with the mode assessments of the experts in **Table 1**.

Row	Parents			Teamwork				
	Autonomy	**Cohesion**	**Collaboration**	**VL**	**L**	**M**	**H**	**VH**
1	VL	VL	VL	X				
2	VL	VL	VH			X		
3	VL	VH	VH				X	
4	VH	VH	VH					X
5	VH	VH	VL				X	
6	VH	VL	VL		X			
7	VH	VL	VH				X	
8	VL	VH	VL				X	

Table 1.
Mode assessments for teamwork, checkmarks indicate the mode assessment of the expert.

First, let us consider the rows 1 and 4, where all the parent nodes are in the highest and lowest states respectively. As can be seen in **Table 1**, when o all the parent nodes are in the lowest or highest states, the mode of the child node is also the lowest or highest state. Such a probability distribution can be obtained by any of the weighted expressions.

Now, let us consider the row 1 as the initial state, rows 2, 6 and 8 indicate that when the state of a single parent node shifts from lowest to highest state the mode of the child node shifts towards the highest state. Similarly, consider row 4 as the initial state, rows 3, 5 and 7 indicate that when the state of a single parent node shifts from highest to lowest state, the mode of the child node also shifts towards the lowest state.

However, it is quite clear that the shift effect is stronger when it occurs from the lowest to highest state. Hence, **Table 1** reveals that the mode of the child node is inclined to go more towards the highest than lowest states which makes the *WMAX* function more suitable to express the distribution expected by the experts.

The process to determine the weights of the parent nodes and the variance parameter is not as straightforward as to determine the weighted expression. There is no guideline in the literature, as far as we know, to aid in this task. Nonetheless, one can use the mode assessments in **Table 1** as a starting point to define the weight of the parent nodes. For instance, considering *WMAX* is the most suitable function to express the probability distribution, let us examine the rows in which the states shift from lowest to highest in **Table 1**.

Finally, let us consider row 1 as the initial state, rows 2, 6 and 8 indicate that the parent nodes have different strengths of influence on the child node. That is, when the parent node *Autonomy* shifts from lowest to highest state the mode of *Teamwork* slightly shifts towards highest states, however, the shift is higher when the state changes in the parent node *Collaboration,* as can be seen, if one compares rows 2 and 6. A similar effect is observed when comparing rows 6 and 8. Hence, it is derived from **Table 1** the following constraint: *Autonomy weight < Collaboration weight < Cohesion weight*. Nevertheless, trial and error are yet necessary to discover suitable values for the weights and the variance parameter.

This method solves the magnitude problem of constructing NPT in complex Bayesian networks. On the other hand, a drawback to this method is that the domain context needs to fit a pattern that can be modeled by one of the weighted expressions. This solution has been validated through case studies in different real-world domains, such as human resources management in software projects [24], software quality forecasting [25], air traffic control [26] and operational management [27].

5.2 WSA

In [8] the WSA method is proposed. This work introduced the concept of compatible parental configuration. The availability heuristic and the simulation heuristic are the base for this concept. As previously stated, the availability heuristic operates under the assumption that is easier to remember events that are more likely to occur. The simulation heuristic, in turn, operates according to which people determine the probability of an event based on how easy it is to simulate it mentally.

To formally define the concept of compatible parental configuration, we take as a basis the work of [28]. Superscript is used to represent the states of a node and subscript to differentiate the parent-nodes. Therefore, consider that for Y_i is assigned an arbitrary state y_i^v , that is, $Y_i = y_i^v$, since Y_j is another parent node, such that Y_j is considered compatible with $Y_i = y_i^v$ only when Y_j is in the state y_j^w which is most likely, according to the expert's knowledge, to coexist with $Y_i = y_i^v$. Hence, we use the notation $Comp\left[Y_i = y_i^v\right]$ to represent the set of states that are compatible with $Y_i = y_i^v$ for all parent nodes.

$$Comp\left[Y_i = y_i^v\right] = \left\{y_j^w, \forall j \neq i \,\middle|\, \max_{w=1...|Y_j|} P\left(y_j^w | y_i^v\right)\right\} \quad (6)$$

The compatible parental configurations are captured during the elicitation process by asking the domain experts to choose off the top of their head a plausible combination of states for each $Comp\left[Y_i = y_i^v\right]$, which, theoretically, are easier to simulate and therefore, prone to more realistic probabilities. Hence, it is elicited from experts the probability distributions for all compatible parental configuration and relative weights. The NPT is calculated using a weighted sum algorithm [8] which takes these probability distributions and weights as input. The input data of the algorithm is obtained from the experts' knowledge, as follows:

1. relative weight (between zero and one) for each parent node, denoting its degree of influence on the child node $w_1, ..., w_n$;

2. $k_1 + ... + k_n$ probability distributions of X for compatible parental configurations.

$$p\left(x^l | y_1^{v_1}, y_2^{v_2}, ..., y_n^{v_n}\right) = \sum_{i=1}^{n} w_j p\left(x^l | Comp\left(Y_j = y_j^{v_j}\right)\right) \quad (7)$$

where w is the relative weight of the parent node, $l = 0, 1, ..., m$ and $v_j = 1, 2, ..., k_j$. A constraint must be observed: the sum of all the relative weights (i.e., of all parent nodes) must be exactly one. A weight equal to zero indicates that the parent node has no influence on the child node and therefore can be omitted from the relation. Conversely, a relative weight equal to one indicates that the parent node is the only determinant of the conditional probabilities on the child node.

For instance, let us consider the Bayesian network shown in **Figure 2** where we wish to assess teamwork. For the sake of simplicity let us say that all the parents have the states "Low", "Medium" and "High" instead of the five states from the original example. With WSA 3×3 distributions are needed to construct a complete NPT against 3^3 in case of manual elicitation. Starting with the parent Y_1, let us say that the domain expert subjectively interprets the compatible parental configurations as an equivalence relation as follows:

$$\{Comp(Y_1 = s)\} \equiv \{Comp(Y_2 = s)\} \equiv \{Comp(Y_3 = s)\}, \text{ for } s = l, m, h \tag{8}$$

When the domain expert provides 3 probability distributions over the node Y_1 then all 3×3 distributions for compatible parental configurations are obtained. To generate the NPT, the expert must assign relative weights to the parents to quantify the relative strengths of their influence on the child node. Let us say that the expert interprets *Autonomy* and *Cohesion* as having the same influence strength on the child node, and *Collaboration* as three times more important than *Cohesion* or *Autonomy*. Hence, assigning the following weights: $w_1 = .2$, $w_2 = .2$, $w_3 = .6$.

With the weights and 3 probability distributions over the node Y_1 as inputs, the weighted sum algorithm calculates all the 3^3 distributions required to populate the NPT. On the other hand, let us say that Eq. (8) is not satisfied, then all the 3×3 probability distributions must be elicited.

In such a case, the probability of *Teamwork (X)* = "Low" conditioned to *Autonomy (Y_1)* = "Low", *Cohesion (Y_2)* = "Medium", and *Collaboration (Y_3)* = "High" would be given by:

$$\begin{aligned} p(X = l | Y_1 = l, Y_2 = m, Y_3 = h) = w_1 p(X = l | \{Comp(Y_1 = l)\} \\ + w_2 p(X = l | \{Comp(Y_2 = m)\} \\ + w_3 p(X = l | \{Comp(Y_3 = h)\} \end{aligned} \tag{9}$$

This summarizes the WSA method, for an in-depth description please check [8]. Unfortunately, [8] do not describe how to deal with situations where the expert cannot select a single compatible parental configuration. Hence, an extension to this method is proposed by [29] to deal with such situations by averaging the probabilities of valid compatible parental configurations that experts might select.

5.3 AHP

Although the direct assessment of probabilities in the construction of NPT is feasible for small Bayesian networks and relatively simple domains, for medium to large networks the complexity and burden for experts grows substantially. As the number of parents and states increase, the more difficult it becomes for experts to reason about conditional probabilities with multiple parents and multiple combinations of states at once, and the more susceptible it becomes to biases and inaccuracies [11].

In [11] it is proposed a systematic approach for generating conditional probabilities of nodes with multiple parents. It is an adaptation of the AHP method for the task of probability elicitation and semiautomatic generation of NPT where the expert only needs to provide probability assessments (i.e., indirect) conditioned on single parents. In this approach, the probability assessments are extracted from pairwise judgments of the states. The NPT is generated through the product of the probabilities of the child node conditioned on single parents.

Before using the proposed method [11] it is required to define an agreed upon scale to perform the pairwise judgments over the states of the node. Saaty's scale [30] can be used for this purpose or a custom one can be created. A good example of how to obtain a scale can be consulted in [19] in which four successive experiments were performed to generate a scale with numbers and words. The Saaty's scale has nine values as seen in **Table 2**.

Scale	Definition	Explanation
1	Equal likely	Event A and evet B are equal likely
2	Weak or slight	
3	Moderate more likely	Event A is moderate more likely than event B
4	Moderate plus	
5	Strong more likely	Event A is Strong more likely than event B
6	Strong plus	
7	Very strong more likely	Event A is very strong more likely than event B
8	Very, very strong	
9	Extremely more likely	Event A is extremely more likely than event B

Table 2.
Scale for the pairwise comparisons.

For a better understanding of the method, we substitute the original terminology used in the AHP for terms more appropriate to the probability context. Thus, the term *attribute* is replaced by *event* and the term *importance* is replaced by *likelihood*. To obtain prior probabilities pairwise comparisons of all states of the node are performed. Since each state is compared to every other state we can assemble a comparison matrix. In **Figure 9** we see an example of a comparison matrix used to define prior probabilities of a node.

In the above matrix, $a_{ij}(i = 1, 2, ..., n; j = 1, 2, ..., n)$ is specified by the question "comparing the state x^{s_i} with x^{s_j}, which is more likely and how more likely?". Once we have filled the values for a_{ij} we can find the values of a_{ji} by calculating the inverse of a_{ij}, i.e., $1/a_{ij}$. The final result is a reciprocal matrix with all elements in the diagonal equal to 1, that is, $a_{ii} = 1$ for all i.

The relative priority of x^{s_i} is obtained from the maximum eigenvector $\omega = (\omega_1, \omega_2, ..., \omega_n)^T$ of the matrix $(a_{ij})_{n\ x\ n}$ and the consistency of the matrix is the consistency ratio $CR = CI/RI$, where CI is the consistency index, defined by $(\lambda_{max} - n)/(n - 1)$ where λ_{max} is the maximum eigenvalue corresponding to ω, and RI is the random index given by **Table 3**. A comparison matrix with CR less than 0.10 is considered acceptable [11]. Although [31] has observed that this threshold may be inappropriate for the purpose of evaluating probabilities. Since the sum of

	x^{s_1}	x^{s_2}	x^{s_n}	ω
x^{s_1}	a_{11}	a_{12}	a_{1n}	ω_1
x^{s_2}	a_{21}	a_{22}	a_{2n}	ω_2
x^{s_n}	a_{n1}	a_{n2}	a_{nn}	ω_n

Figure 9.
Comparison matrix for prior probability elicitation of a node X.

n	1	2	3	4	5	6	7	8	9
RI	0	0	0.58	0.90	1.12	1.24	1.32	1.41	1.45

Table 3.
Random consistency index where n is the number of states.

all elements in ω is 1 and the ith element ω_i represents the relative importance of the state x^{s_i}, ω_i is now interpreted as the prior probability of the state x^{s_i}, that is, $P(x^{s_i}) = \omega_i$.

Similarly, to obtain the probabilities of a node X with a single parent Y we estimate $P(x^{s_i}, |y^{s_j})$. In **Figure 10** we see the resulting matrix when node $Y = y^{s_j}$:

In the above matrix $a_{pq}(p = 1, 2, ..., n; q = 1, 2, ..., n)$ is specified by questions such as "if the node Y is in the y^{s_j} state, comparing the states x^{s_i} and x^{s_j} of the child node X, which one is more likely and how more likely? ". After obtaining $\omega_{ij}(i = 1, ..., n)$ we have $P(X = x^{s_i}|Y = y^{s_j}) = \omega_{ij}$. The number of matrices needed to obtain $\omega_{ij}(i = 1, 2, ..., n; j = 1, 2, ..., m)$ is equal to the number of states of Y. The obtained results compose the NPT of a child node X conditioned to the states of a parent Y, as shown in **Figure 11**.

The approach to generate the conditional probabilities for multi-parent nodes is based on [32], which states that when a node A in a Bayesian network has two parents B and C, its conditional probability in B and C can be approximated by $P(A|B, C) = \propto P(A|B)P(A|C)$ where $\propto$ is a normalizing factor that ensures that $\propto \sum_{a \in A} P(a|B, C) = 1$. Hence, to generate the complete NPT Eq. (10) is applied:

$$P(X = x^{s_i} \,|Y_1 = y_1^{s_i}, Y_2 = y_2^{s_i}, ..., Y_k = y_k^{s_i}) = \propto \prod_{j=1}^{k} P\left(X = x^{s_i}|Y_j = y_j^{s_i}\right) \tag{10}$$

This approach focuses on easing the burden for experts by automatically generating probabilistic distributions of nodes with multiple parents, and consequently, the complete NPT through the calculation of the product of the probabilities conditioned on single parents. Thus, the expert assesses the probabilities of a particular child node conditioned to each of its parents, one at a time, and these probabilities are combined to get the node's conditional probability conditional on all its parents.

	x^{S_1}	x^{S_2}	x^{S_n}	ω_x
x^{S_1}	a_{11}	a_{12}	a_{1n}	ω_{1j}
x^{S_2}	a_{21}	a_{22}	a_{2n}	ω_{2j}
x^{S_n}	a_{n1}	a_{n2}	a_{nn}	ω_{nj}

Figure 10.
Comparison matrix of a node X conditioned on a single parent Y in the state y^{s_j}.

		States of Y		
		y^{S_1}	y^{S_2}	y^{S_m}
	x^{S_1}	ω_{11}	ω_{12}	ω_{1m}
States of X	x^{S_2}	ω_{21}	ω_{22}	ω_{1m}
	x^{S_n}	ω_{n1}	ω_{n2}	ω_{nm}

Figure 11.
Resulting NPT for a single parent node.

In [31] a similar method is proposed, also based on the AHP, which allow the quantitative evaluation of the inconsistency of experts in the task of probability assessment. The difference of the proposed methods is that in [11] the magnitude problem to construct NPT is reduced with a semiautomatic approach for the generation of the NPT and the cognitive effort is reduced because the experts only need to evaluate, indirectly, probabilistic distributions conditioned on a single parent at a time, whereas in [31] the effort is even greater than the direct elicitation of probabilities. Nonetheless, it is our understanding that the method proposed in [31] can somewhat extend other methods such as the WSA, without causing too much overhead. However, further studies are needed to confirm this.

6. Conclusion

Despite recent popularity, the construction of BN is still a challenging task. One of the main obstacles refers to defining the NPT for large-scale BN. It is possible to automate this process using batch learning, but it requires a database with enough information. In practice, this is not common. The other option is to elicit data from experts, which is unfeasible in most cases due to the number of probabilities required. A third option is to use semiautomatic methods that given an input (i.e., elicited from experts) generates the NPT.

In this chapter, we present three semiautomatic methods, found in an exploratory study through a literature review. These methods help, to a certain extent, to minimize the effects of human biases by reducing the parameters that are required to construct complete NPT. However, these methods are highly reliable on the input data elicited from experts. Therefore, flawed input necessarily produces nonsense output. For this reason, we present one of many probability elicitation techniques as an example, which can improve the input data needed by the semiautomatic methods and reduce the garbage in/garbage out effect.

The biggest problem with elaborated probability elicitation techniques is undoubtedly its cost, which is often greater than the direct elicitation of probabilities. Thus, these methods are not well suited for the construction of large-scale BN, despite been useful to deal with well know biases. However, it is our understanding that the cost to use elaborated probability elicitation techniques is drastically reduced when only is needed to elicit a small fraction of data of what would be necessary for manual definition of NPT. Therefore, the combination of semiautomatic methods and elaborated probability elicitation techniques might help building more reliable BN.

For example, let us consider the WSA method that uses a partial elicited NPT to generate a complete one using the concept of compatible parental configurations, weights of the parents and a weighted sum algorithm. Once the compatible parental configurations have been chosen, its probabilities can be elicited using a sophisticated probability elicitation technique with a rather small overhead. In one way, the probability elicitation technique becomes feasible and, theoretically, the input of the semiautomatic method is improved.

Nonetheless, it is evident that some methods may benefit more from elaborated probability elicitation techniques than others. However, it is still possible to use these techniques even in a method such as RNM. For example, the expert can inform the probabilities rather than the mode of each probabilistic distribution of the combination of extreme states (see **Table 1**). We believe that studies must be carried out to check if combining elaborated probability elicitation techniques with semiautomatic method can indeed improve the construction of large-scale BN.

Author details

João Nunes*, Mirko Barbosa, Luiz Silva, Kyller Gorgônio, Hyggo Almeida and Angelo Perkusich
Federal University of Campina Grande, Paraíba, Brazil

*Address all correspondence to: joaobatista@copin.ufcg.edu.br

References

[1] Fenton NE, Neil M, Caballero JG. Using ranked nodes to model qualitative judgments in Bayesian networks. IEEE Transactions on Knowledge and Data Engineering. 2007;**19**(10):1420-1432

[2] Perkusich M et al. A procedure to detect problems of processes in software development projects using Bayesian networks. Expert Systems with Applications. 2015;**42**(1):437-450

[3] Perkusich M et al. Assisting the continuous improvement of scrum projects using metrics and bayesian networks. Journal of Software: Evolution and Process. 2017;**29**(6):e1835

[4] Lee E, Park Y, Shin JG. Large engineering project risk management using a Bayesian belief network. Expert Systems with Applications. 2009;**36**(3): 5880-5887

[5] De Melo ACV, Sanchez AJ. Software maintenance project delays prediction using Bayesian networks. Expert Systems with Applications. 2008;**34**(2):908-919

[6] Heckerman D. A tutorial on learning with Bayesian networks. In: Learning in Graphical Models. Dordrecht: Springer; 1998. pp. 301-354

[7] Constantinou A, Fenton N. Towards smart-data: Improving predictive accuracy in long-term football team performance. Knowledge-Based Systems. 2017;**124**:93-104

[8] Das B. Generating conditional probabilities for Bayesian networks: Easing the knowledge acquisition problem. arXiv preprint cs/0411034; 2004

[9] Tversky A, Kahneman D. Availability: A heuristic for judging frequency and probability. Cognitive Psychology. 1973;**5**(2):207-232

[10] Kahneman D, Tversky A. The Simulation Heuristic. No. TR-5. Stanford Univ CA Dept of Psychology; 1981

[11] Chin K-S et al. Assessing new product development project risk by Bayesian network with a systematic probability generation methodology. Expert Systems with Applications. 2009;**36**(6):9879-9890

[12] Ben-Gal I. Bayesian networks. Encyclopedia of statistics in quality and reliability. 2008;**1**

[13] Friedman N, Geiger D, Goldszmidt M. Bayesian network classifiers. Machine Learning. 1997;**29**(2–3): 131-163

[14] Pearl J, Russell S. Bayesian networks. In: Handbook of Brain Theory and Neural Networks. Cambridge, MA, USA: MIT Press. 1998:149-153

[15] Freire A et al. A Bayesian networks-based approach to assess and improve the teamwork quality of agile teams. Information and Software Technology. 2018;**100**:119-132

[16] Tversky A, Kahneman D. Judgment under uncertainty: Heuristics and biases. Science. 1974;**185**(4157): 1124-1131

[17] Renooij S. Probability elicitation for belief networks: Issues to consider. The Knowledge Engineering Review. 2001; **16**(3):255-269

[18] Chesley GR. Subjective probability elicitation techniques: A performance comparison. Journal of Accounting Research. 1978;**16**(2):225-241

[19] Renooij S, Witteman C. Talking Probabilities: Communicating Probabilistic Information with Words

and Numbers. International Journal of Approximate Reasoning. 1999;**22**:169-194

[20] Van Der Gaag LC et al. How to elicit many probabilities. In: Proceedings of the Fifteenth Conference on Uncertainty in Artificial Intelligence. San Francisco, CA, USA: Morgan Kaufmann Publishers Inc. 1999. pp. 647-654

[21] Van Der Gaag LC et al. Probabilities for a probabilistic network: A case study in oesophageal cancer. Artificial Intelligence in Medicine. 2002;**25**(2): 123-148

[22] Nunes Joao et al. An algorithm to define the node probability functions of Bayesian networks based on ranked nodes. International Journal of Engineering Trends and Technology (IJETT). 2017;**52**(3):151-157

[23] Laitila P, Virtanen K. Improving construction of conditional probability tables for ranked nodes in Bayesian networks. IEEE Transactions on Knowledge and Data Engineering. 2016; **28**(7):1691-1705

[24] Fenton N et al. Making resource decisions for software projects. In: Proceedings of the 26th International Conference on Software Engineering. IEEE Computer Society; 2004. pp. 397-406

[25] Fenton N et al. Predicting software defects in varying development lifecycles using Bayesian nets. Information and Software Technology. 2007;**49**(1):32-43

[26] Neil M, Malcolm B, Shaw R. Modelling an air traffic control environment using Bayesian belief networks. In: 21st International System Safety Conference; Ottawa, Ontario, Canada. p. 2003

[27] Neil M, Fenton N, Tailor M. Using Bayesian networks to model expected and unexpected operational losses. Risk Analysis. 2005;**25**(4):963-972

[28] Mendes E et al. Towards improving decision making and estimating the value of decisions in value-based software engineering: The VALUE framework. Software Quality Journal. 2018;**26**(2):607-656

[29] Baker S, Mendes E. Assessing the weighted sum algorithm for automatic generation of probabilities in Bayesian networks. In: Information and Automation (ICIA), 2010 IEEE International Conference on. IEEE; 2010. pp. 867-873

[30] Saaty TL. How to make a decision: The analytic hierarchy process. Interfaces. 1994;**24**(6):19-43

[31] Monti S, Carenini G. Dealing with the expert inconsistency in probability elicitation. IEEE Transactions on Knowledge and Data Engineering. 2000;**12**(4):499-508

[32] Kim J, Pearl J. A computational model for causal and diagnostic reasoning in inference systems. In: International Joint Conference on Artificial Intelligence. San Francisco, CA, USA: Morgan Kaufmann Publishers Inc. 1983;1:190-193

Chapter 3

Classic and Bayesian Tree-Based Methods

Amal Saki Malehi and Mina Jahangiri

Abstract

Tree-based methods are nonparametric techniques and machine-learning methods for data prediction and exploratory modeling. These models are one of valuable and powerful tools among data mining methods and can be used for predicting different types of outcome (dependent) variable: (e.g., quantitative, qualitative, and time until an event occurs (survival data)). Tree model is called classification tree/regression tree/survival tree based on the type of outcome variable. These methods have some advantages over against traditional statistical methods such as generalized linear models (GLMs), discriminant analysis, and survival analysis. Some of these advantages are: without requiring to determine assumptions about the functional form between outcome variable and predictor (independent) variables, invariant to monotone transformations of predictor variables, useful for dealing with nonlinear relationships and high-order interactions, deal with different types of predictor variable, ease of interpretation and understanding results without requiring to have statistical experience, robust to missing values, outliers, and multicollinearity. Several classic and Bayesian tree algorithms are proposed for classification and regression trees, and in this chapter, we provide a review of these algorithms and appropriate criteria for determining the predictive performance of them.

Keywords: classic classification trees, Bayesian classification trees, classic regression trees, Bayesian regression trees

1. Introduction

Different parametric traditional models are proposed for predicting different types of outcome variable (e.g., (quantitative, qualitative, and survival data)) and exploratory modeling. These parametric models are: generalized linear models (GLMs) [1], discriminant analysis [2], and survival analysis [3]. Also, different nonparametric methods are proposed for data prediction and some of these methods are: classic and Bayesian tree-based methods, support vector machines [4], artificial neural networks [5], multivariate adaptive regression splines [6], K-nearest neighbor [7], Bayesian networks [8], and generalized additive models (GAMs) [9].

Classic and Bayesian tree-based methods are defined as machine-learning methods for data prediction and exploratory modeling. These methods are supervised methods and are one of powerful and most popular tools for classification and prediction. These methods have some good advantages over traditional statistical methods and these advantages are [10–12]:

- easy to interpret due to display result as graphically;
- understanding result without requiring to have statistical experience;
- deal with high-dimensional dataset and large dataset;
- without requiring to determine assumptions about the functional form of the data;
- deal with nonlinear relationships and high-order interactions;
- invariant to monotone transformations of predictor variables;
- robust to missing values;
- robust to outliers;
- robust to multicollinearity;
- extract homogeneous subgroups of observations.

Tree-based methods have been used in different sciences such as medical studies and epidemiologic studies [13–17]. In these studies, tree models are used for determining risk factors of diseases and identifying high-risk and low-risk subgroups of patients. Tree methods can determine subgroups of patients that need to different diagnostic tests or treatment strategies, indeed these methods are useful for subgroup analysis [18, 19].

Several classic and Bayesian tree algorithms are proposed for classification trees, regression trees, and survival trees. These tree algorithms classify observations into a finite homogeneous subgroups based on predictor variables. Tree model is called classification tree, regression tree, and survival tree, if the outcome variable is a quantitative variable, qualitative variable, and survival data, respectively. Tree-based methods extract homogeneous subgroups of data by a recursively partitioning process and then fit a constant model or a parametric model such as linear regression, Poisson regression, and logistic regression for data prediction within these subgroups. Finally, this process is displayed graphically like a tree structure and this advantage is one of the attractive properties of tree models [20].

In this chapter, we review classic and Bayesian classification and regression tree approaches. Owing to space limitation, Bayesian approaches are discussed more, because this chapter provides the first comprehensive review of Bayesian classification and regression trees.

We begin with a discussion of the steps for tree generating of classic classification and regression trees in Section 2. We mention classic classification trees on Section 3. Section 4 provides a review on classic regression trees. Section 5 contains a discussion of treed generalized linear models. A review of Bayesian classification and regression trees is provided in Section 6. Appropriate criteria for determining the predictive performance of tree-based methods are mentioned in Section 7, and Section 8 presents the conclusion.

2. Classic classification and regression trees

In a dataset with an outcome variable Y and P-vector of predictor variables as $X = \{x_1, \ldots, x_p\}$, recursive partitioning process of tree generating for classic tree algorithms has several main steps and these steps are: tree growing step, stopping the tree growth step, and tree pruning step. Some of the tree algorithms use two steps (tree growing and stopping the tree growth) for tree generating. These steps are as follows:

2.1 Tree growing

Tree growing step is the first step for tree generating and this step is performed using a binary recursive partitioning process based on a splitting function that this binary tree subdivides the predictor variable space. Tree growth begins at the root node and this node is the top-most node in the tree and includes all observations in the learning dataset. Tree grows by either splitting or not splitting each node of tree (each node contains a subset of learning dataset) into two child nodes or left and right daughter nodes using splitting rules for classifying observations into homogeneous subgroups in terms of outcome variable. Splitting rules for classifying observations are selected using some splitting functions. Binary recursive partitioning process continues until none of the nodes can split or stopping rule of tree growth is reached. We will mention these stopping rules. Binary recursive partitioning process splits each node of tree into only two nodes, but some of tree algorithms can generate multiway splits [20].

In tree growing process, nodes that split are called internal node and otherwise are called terminal node. Each internal node includes a subset of dataset and all internal nodes in tree are parent of their subnodes. Each sample of learning dataset is placed in one of the terminal nodes of tree, and the tree size is equal to the number of terminal nodes of tree. Each node of tree is splitted based on a splitting rule for classifying observations into left and right daughter nodes. If chosen splitting rule is based on a quantitative predictor variable, then observations divide based on $\{x_i \leq s\}$ or $\{x_i > s\}$ into left and right nodes, respectively (s: an observed value of quantitative predictor variable). If chosen splitting rule is based on a qualitative predictor variable, then observations divide based on $\{x_i \in C\}$ or $\{x_i \notin C\}$ into left and right nodes, respectively (C: a category subset of qualitative predictor variable). Many splitting rules can be in each node and all possible splitting rules must be checked for determining best splitting rule using a goodness of fit criterion. This criterion shows the degree of homogeneity in the daughter nodes, and homogeneity is computed using a splitting function and best splitting rule has the highest goodness of fit criterion [20].

Several splitting functions are proposed for classification trees and some of them are [21]: Entropy, Information Gain, Gini Index, Error Classification, Gain Ratio, Marshal Correction, Chi-square, Twoing, Distance Measure [22], Kolmogorov-Smirnov [23, 24], and AUC-splitting [25]. Also, several studies compared the performance of splitting functions [21, 26, 27].

In tree growing process, a predicted value is assigned to each node. Data prediction in classification trees such as C4.5 [28], CART [29], CHAID [30], FACT [31], QUEST [32], CRUISE [33], and GUIDE [34] is based on fitting a constant model like the proportion of the categories of outcome variable at each node of tree. CRUISE algorithm also can fit bivariate linear discriminant models [35] and GUIDE algorithm also can fit kernel density model and nearest neighbor model at each node of tree [34]. All mentioned classification trees except C4.5 tree algorithm accept user-defined misclassification cost, and all except CHAID and C4.5 methods accept user-defined class prior probabilities.

Data prediction in regression trees such as AID [36], M5 [37], CART [29], and GUIDE [38] is based on fitting a constant model like the mean of outcome variable at each node of tree. M5 also can fit linear regression model and GUIDE can fit models such as linear regression model and polynomial model.

2.2 Stopping the tree growth step

Stopping the tree growth step is the second step for tree generating. Tree growth is continued until it is possible, and several rules are proposed for stopping the tree growth and we mention some of them [29, 39]:

- There is only one observation in the terminal nodes.
- All observations in the terminal nodes are belong to a category of outcome variable.
- Node splitting is impossible, because all observations in each of terminal nodes have the same distribution of predictor variables.
- Determining a user-specified minimum threshold for goodness-of-fit criterion of splitting rules.
- There is the number of observations less than a user-specified minimum threshold in the terminal nodes.
- Determining a user-specified maximum for depth of tree.

2.3 Tree pruning step

Tree pruning step is the third step for tree generating and this step is one of the main steps for tree generating. Tree algorithm produces a large maximal tree or saturated tree (the nodes of this tree cannot split any further, because terminal nodes have one observation or observations are belong to a category of outcome variable within each terminal node) and then prunes it to avoid overfitting. In this step, a sequence of trees is generated and each tree in this sequence is an extension of previous trees. Finally, an optimal tree is selected among the trees of sequence based on having lowest cost of misclassification (for classification tree) and lowest estimated prediction error (for regression tree) [29].

Several methods are proposed for tree pruning and some of these methods are [39, 40]: cost-complexity pruning, reduced error pruning, pessimistic error pruning, minimum error pruning, error-based pruning, critical value pruning, and minimum description length pruning [41]. Also, several studies compared the performance of pruning methods [39, 40].

3. Classic classification trees

Several classic classification tree approaches are proposed to classify observations, and data prediction in a dataset contains a qualitative outcome variable Y with K categories or classes and P-vector of predictor variables as $X = \{x_1, \ldots, x_p\}$. We review some of these classification tree algorithms and these algorithms are: THAID, CHAID, CART, ID3, FACT, C4.5, QUEST, CRUISE, and GUIDE. Also, we only checked software programs such as SPSS, STATISTICA, TANAGRA, WEKA, CART, and R for being these tree methods and available software programs are mentioned for each model. Owing to space limitation, we only mention the name of other classification tree algorithms and these algorithms are: SLIQ [42], SPRINT [43], RainForest [44], OC1 [45], T1 [46], CAL5 [47, 48], and CTREE [49].

3.1 THAID (theta automatic interaction detector)

THAID classification tree algorithm is developed by Messenger and Mandell in 1972 and is the first published classification tree algorithm [50]. This tree algorithm only deals with qualitative predictor variables and uses a greedy search approach for tree generating. Splitting function in THAID algorithm is based on the number of cases in categories of outcome variable, and splitting rule for node splitting is selected based on minimizing the total impurity of new two daughter nodes. THAID method does not use any pruning method, and tree growth is continued until decrease in impurity is higher than a minimum user-specified limit.

3.2 CHAID (chi-square automatic interaction detector) and exhaustive CHAID

CHAID classification tree algorithm is developed by Kass in 1980 and this algorithm is a descendant of THAID tree algorithm [30]. This algorithm can generate multiway splits and tree-growing process including three steps: merging, splitting, and stopping. Also, continuous predictor variables must be categorized, because CHAID only accepts qualitative predictor variables in tree generating process. CHAID algorithm uses significance tests with a Bonferroni correction as splitting function, and best splitting rule is selected based on having lowest significance probability. This tree algorithm generates biased splits and deals with missing values. CHAID algorithm is implemented in these software programs: SPSS, STATISTICA, and R (CHAID package).

Exhaustive CHAID algorithm is proposed by Biggs et al. in 1991 and this algorithm is an improved CHAID method. The splitting and stopping steps of this algorithm are the same as the CHAID algorithm, and it just changed to improve merging [51].

3.3 CART (classification and regression trees)

The classic CART model was developed by Breiman et al. in 1984 and this model is a binary tree algorithm [29]. CART algorithm is one of the best known classic classification and regression trees for data mining. CART algorithm generates a classification tree using a binary recursive partitioning, and tree generating process in this algorithm contains four steps: (1) tree growing: tree growth is based on a greedy search algorithm that CART algorithm grows tree by sequentially choosing splitting rules. This classification tree algorithm provides three splitting functions for choosing splitting rules, and these splitting functions are: entropy, Gini index, and twoing. (2) tree growing process continues until none of the nodes can split, and a large maximal tree is generated. (3) tree pruning: CART uses cost-complexity pruning method for tree pruning to avoid overfitting and to obtain "right-sized" trees. This pruning method generates several subtrees or a sequence of pruned trees, and each tree in this sequence is an extension of the previous trees. (4) best tree selection: CART uses independent test dataset or cross-validation to estimate the prediction error (misclassification cost) of each tree and then selects the best tree from sequence of trees with lowest estimated prediction error.

CART can generate linear combination splits and uses surrogate splits for dealing with missing values, and also, these surrogate splits are used to measure an importance score for predictor variables. This best known classic tree algorithm suffers from some problems such as greediness, instability, and bias in split rule selection [52]. CART is available at these software programs: CART, R (rpart package), SPSS, STATISTICA, WEKA, and TANAGRA.

3.4 ID3 (Iterative Dichotomiser 3)

ID3 classification tree algorithm is proposed by Quinlan in 1986 [53]. This algorithm uses a greedy algorithm using information gain as splitting function and this splitting function is based on entropy splitting criterion and best splitting rule has highest information gain. ID3 does not use any pruning methods, and tree growth process is continued until all observations in the terminal nodes are belong to a category of outcome variable and/or best information gain is near to zero. This algorithm only deals with qualitative predictor variables (if dataset contains quantitative predictor variables, they must be categorized). Also, ID3 algorithm cannot impute missing values, and this method like CART model suffers from selection bias, because ID3 algorithm favors the predictor variables with more values for node splitting of tree. ID3 is implemented in these software programs: WEKA and TANAGRA.

3.5 FACT (Fast and Accurate Classification Tree)

FACT classification tree algorithm was introduced by Loh and Vanichsetakul in 1988 [31]. In this algorithm, variable selection for node splitting based on quantitative predictor variable is based on having the largest F-statistics of analysis of variance (ANOVA), and then, linear discriminant analysis is used to determine split point for this variable. FACT model transforms qualitative predictor variables into ordered variables in two steps (first step: these variables are transformed into dummy vectors, second step: these vectors are projected onto the largest discriminant coordinate). FACT generates unbiased splits when dataset contains only quantitative predictor variables. Also, it, unlike other classification tree methods (C4.5, CART, QUEST, GUIDE and CRUISE), does not use any pruning methods, and tree growing is stopped when stopping rule is reached. FACT can deal with missing values and missing values of quantitative and qualitative predictor variables are imputed at each node by the means and modes of the non-missing values, respectively.

3.6 C4.5

C4.5 classification tree algorithm is developed by Quinlan in 1993 and this algorithm is an extension of ID3 tree algorithm [28]. This algorithm uses a greedy algorithm using gain ratio as splitting function and generates biased splits. C4.5, unlike ID3 method, deals with quantitative and qualitative predictor variables and also, deals with missing values. In this tree method, split of quantitative predictor variable is binary split and split of qualitative predictor variable is multiway split (a branch is created for each category of qualitative predictor variable). Pruning method used in this algorithm is error-based pruning method. C4.5 is available at these software programs: R (Rweka package), WEKA, TANAGRA, and also can obtain from: http://www.rulequest.com/Personal/. Also, J4.8 tree algorithm is Java implementation of the C4.5 algorithm in WEKA software.

3.7 QUEST (Quick, Unbiased, and Efficient Statistical Tree)

Quest classification tree algorithm is developed by Loh and Shih in 1997, and this model generates binary splits [32]. This method, unlike other classification algorithms such as CART and THAID, does not use exhaustive search algorithm (because these algorithms suffer from variable selection bias) and so improves computational cost and variable selection bias. Quest tree method uses statistical test for selecting variable splitting and then variable with smallest significance probability is selected to split node of tree. This method uses F-statistics of analysis of variance (ANOVA) for quantitative predictor variables and chi-square test for qualitative predictor variables. After determining variable, an exhaustive search is implemented to find the best split point and QUEST method uses quadratic discriminant analysis for selecting split point. For determining split point of a qualitative variable, values of this variable must be transforming like method used in FACT algorithm.

Quest like CART can generate linear combination splits and uses cost-complexity pruning method for tree pruning. Missing values of quantitative and qualitative predictor variable are imputed at each node by the means and modes of the non-missing values, respectively. Software for QUEST algorithm can be obtained from: www.stat.wisc.edu/~loh/.

3.8 CRUISE (Classification Rule with Unbiased Interaction Selection and Estimation)

CRUISE tree algorithm was introduced by Kim and Loh in 2001, and this algorithm, unlike other classification tree algorithms (CART and QUEST), generates multiway splits [33]. CRUISE method is free of selection bias and can detect local interactions. Two methods of variable selection are used in this tree model and these methods are: 1D (similar to the method used in QUEST method) and 2D. CRUISE method like CART and QUEST can generate linear combination splits and uses cost-complexity pruning method for tree pruning. Also, a bivariate linear discriminant model can fit instead of constant model in each node of tree [35]. CRUISE uses several methods for imputing missing values in the learning dataset and dataset used for tree pruning. Software for CRUISE algorithm can be obtained from: www.stat.wisc.edu/~loh/.

3.9 GUIDE (Generalized, Unbiased, Interaction Detection, and Estimation)

GUIDE tree algorithm was introduced by Loh in 2009, and this method is an evolution of FACT, QUEST, and CRUISE algorithms and improves the weaknesses of these algorithms [34]. It like QUEST and CRUISE generates unbiased binary splits and can perform splits on combinations of two predictor variables at a time. Also, GUIDE like QUEST and CRUISE methods performs the two-step approach based on significance tests for splitting each node. GUIDE uses a chi-squared test of independence of each independent variable versus dependent variable on the data in the node and computes its significance probability. It chooses the variable associated with the smallest significance probability and finds a split point that minimizes the sum of Gini indexes and uses it to split the node into two daughter nodes.

GUIDE method uses cost-complexity pruning method for tree pruning (this method is used in other tree algorithms such CART, QUEST, and CRUISE). It deals with missing values and assigns them as a separate category. Also, this tree method can compute importance score for predictor variables and can use nearest neighbor model and bivariate kernel density instead of constant model in the nodes of tree. Software for GUIDE algorithm can be obtained from: www.stat.wisc.edu/~loh/.

3.10 Classification tree algorithms for ordinal outcome variable

Several tree methods are proposed for predicting an ordinal outcome variable. Twoing splitting function is extended by Breiman et al. for using classification tree for ordinal outcome variable [29] and also Piccarreta extended Gini-Simpson criterion for this case [54]. Archer proposed a package in R software (rpartOrdinal package) and this package contains some splitting functions for tree generating for predicting an ordinal outcome variable [55]. Also, Galimberti et al. developed a package in R software (rpartScore package) that overcomes some problems of rpartOrdinal package [56]. Tutz and Hechenbichler extended ensemble tree methods such as bagging and boosting for analyzing an ordinal outcome variable [57]. For study about other approaches, refer to Refs. [49, 57–60].

3.11 Classification tree algorithms for imbalanced datasets

In an imbalanced dataset, one of the classes of outcome variable has fewer samples than other classes and this class is rare. In real applications such as medical diagnosis studies, this rare class is the interest for analyzing. Due to the skew distribution of classes, most classification tree algorithms predict all samples of rare class as a class with more samples. Indeed, these models are not robust to unbalance between classes and have good diagnostic performances only on the class with more samples. Several remedies have been proposed to solve this problem for using classification tree algorithms on the imbalanced datasets. Some of these remedies are: sampling methods (undersampling, oversampling, and synthetic minority oversampling technique (SMOTE)), cost-sensitive learning, class confidence proportion decision tree [61], and Hellinger distance decision trees [62]. Ganganwar in 2012 provides a review of classification algorithms for imbalanced datasets [63].

4. Classic regression trees

Several classic regression trees are proposed to classify observations, and data prediction in a dataset contains a quantitative outcome variable Y and P-vector of predictor variables as $X = \{x_1, \ldots, x_p\}$. We review some of these regression tree algorithms and these algorithms are AID, CART, M5, and GUIDE. Also, we only checked software programs such as SPSS, STATISTICA, TANAGRA, WEKA, CART, and R for being these tree algorithms, and available software programs are mentioned for each model. Owing to space limitation, we only mention the reference of other classification tree algorithms and refer to references for study about other regression tree approaches [49, 64, 65]. Also, for Poisson regression trees, refer to Refs. [66–69].

4.1 AID (automatic interaction detector)

AID regression tree algorithm is proposed by Morgan and Sonquist in 1963, and this algorithm is the first published regression tree algorithm [36]. It generates binary splits and piecewise constant models. This algorithm uses a greedy search for tree generating and a splitting rule is selected based on minimizing the total sum of the square errors. AID suffers from bias in variable selection and this method does not use any pruning method and tree growing is stopped when the reduction in total sum of the square errors is less than a predetermined value.

4.2 CART

CART algorithm considers both classification and regression trees, and tree-generating process in CART algorithm for generating a regression tree is like classification tree [29]. But another splitting function is used to choosing splitting rules of regression tree, and this function is least squares deviation. Also, CART algorithm for selecting best regression subtree uses independent test dataset or cross-validation to estimate the prediction error (sum of squared differences between the observations and predictions) of each tree to select the best tree from sequence of trees with lowest estimated prediction error. CART algorithm for regression tree generating like classification tree uses surrogate splits for imputing missing values and can generate linear combination splits. CART is available at these software programs: CART, R (rpart package), STATISTICA, WEKA, and TANAGRA.

4.3 M5

M5 tree algorithm is proposed by Quinlan in 1992 and this algorithm like AID and CART methods generates a piecewise constant model and then fits a linear regression model in nodes of tree [37]. M5 improves the prediction accuracy of tree algorithm using linear regression model at nodes and deals with missing values. Also, this method like CART algorithm uses least-squares deviation as splitting function and can generate multiway splits. In M5, smoothing technique is used after tree pruning, and this technique improves the accuracy predictions. Wang and Witten in 1996 proposed M5′ tree algorithm, and this method is based on M5 method [70]. This method is available at these software programs: WEKA and R (RWeka package).

4.4 GUIDE

GUIDE method is introduced by Loh in 2002, and it generates unbiased binary splits [38]. This method uses a regression model at each node of tree and calculates the residuals. Then, residuals are transformed to a binary variable based on the sign of them (positive or negative), and algorithm is followed like algorithm used for classification tree. This tree method like method used for classification tree uses missing value category and can compute importance score for predictor variables. GUIDE can fit models such as linear regression model and polynomial model instead of constant model in the nodes of tree. Software for GUIDE method can be obtained from: www.stat.wisc.edu/~loh/.

5. Treed generalized linear models

Some of tree-based methods such as CART, QUEST, C4.5, and CHAID fit a constant model in the nodes of tree, thus a large tree is generated, and this tree has hard interpretation. Treed models, unlike conventional tree models, partition data into subsets and then fit a parametric model such as linear regression, Poisson regression, and logistic regression instead of using constant models (mean or proportion) for data prediction. Treed models generate smaller trees in comparison to tree models. Also, treed models can be a good alternative for traditional parametric models such as GLMs, when these parametric models cannot estimate relationship between outcome variable and predictor variables across a dataset. Several tree algorithms are developed that fit parametric models into terminal nodes, and to study these algorithms, refer to Refs. [71–77].

6. Bayesian classification and regression trees

The classic CART algorithm was developed by Breiman et al. in 1984, and this model is one of the best known classic classification and regression trees for data mining. But this algorithm suffers from some problems such as greediness, instability, and bias in split rule selection. CART generates a tree by using a greedy search algorithm, and this search algorithm has disadvantages such as: limit the exploration of tree space, dependence future splits to previous splits, generate optimistic error rates, and the inability of the search to find a global optimum [78]. CART has instability problem, because by resampling or drawing bootstrap samples from dataset may generate tree with different splits [79]. The splitting method in CART model is biased toward predictor variables with many distinct values and more missing values [80, 81].

Several tree models are suggested to solve these problems and these remedial models are ensemble of trees such as Random Forests [82], Bagging [83], Boosting [84], Multiboost [85], and LogitBoost [86] (for solving instability problem), tree algorithms such as CRUISE [33, 35], QUEST [32], GUIDE [34], CTREE [49], and LOTUS [71] (for solving bias in split rule selection problem), and Bayesian tree approaches and evtree algorithm [78] are suggested to solve greediness problem of CART. Also, Bayesian tree approaches can quantify uncertainty, and these approaches explore the tree space more than classic approaches.

Several Bayesian approaches are proposed for tree-based methods [87–98]. In these Bayesian tree approaches like classic tree approaches, a model is called Bayesian classification trees if the outcome variable is a qualitative variable. Also, a model is called Bayesian regression trees if the outcome variable is a quantitative variable. The method of data prediction in these Bayesian approaches is like classic approaches. The method of data prediction for Bayesian classification trees is based on fitting a constant model like the proportion of the outcome variable in the terminal nodes. Data prediction in Bayesian regression tree is based on fitting a constant model like the mean of the outcome variable in the terminal nodes.

Classic tree approaches use only observations for data analysis, but Bayesian approaches combine prior information with observations. Bayesian tree approaches define prior distributions on the components of classic tree approaches and then utilize stochastic search algorithms through Markov chain Monte Carlo (MCMC) algorithms or deterministic search algorithms for exploring tree space [87–98].

Bayesian tree approaches have materials such as prior distribution function, posterior distribution function, data likelihood function, marginal likelihood function, stochastic search algorithm or deterministic search algorithm for exploring tree space, stopping rule of simulation algorithm (if stochastic search algorithms are used to simulate from posterior distribution and explore tree space) and criteria for identify good trees (if model produces several trees). In this section, we review Bayesian tree approaches and also mention the results of published papers based on using these Bayesian algorithms for data analysis.

6.1 BUNTINE's Bayesian classification tree approach

The first Bayesian tree approach for classification tree model was proposed by Buntine in 1992. This proposed approach offers a full Bayesian analysis for classification tree model by using a deterministic search algorithm instead of using a stochastic search algorithm [87]. This model like other classic tree models uses a splitting function for tree growth using Bayesian statistics with similar performance to splitting methods such as Information Gain and Gini. Buntine also like traditional tree models, in order to prevent overfitting model, used Bayesian smoothing and averaging techniques instead of pruning the tree.

In this Bayesian approach, prior distributions are defined on the tree space and data distribution in the terminal nodes of tree (similar priors distributions use for data distribution in the terminal nodes unlike prior distributions considered on the tree space). Buntine showed the superior performance of Bayesian approach in comparison to classic tree algorithms such as CART model of Breiman et al. and C4 model of Quinlan et al. [99] on several datasets [87]. This Bayesian approach may be obtained from: http://ksvanhorn.com/bayes/free-bayes-software.html.

6.2 CGM's Bayesian CART approach

CGM (Chipman, George, McCulloch) proposed a Bayesian approach for CART model by defining prior distributions on the two components of CART model (Θ, T) in 1998, and these components are a binary tree T with $\mathcal{K}$ terminal nodes and parameter set $\Theta = (\theta_1, \theta_2, \ldots, \theta_{\mathcal{K}})$ [89, 91–93]. Indeed, they define prior distributions on tree structure and parameters in terminal nodes. In this approach, following equation is established for joint posterior distribution of components according to Bayes' theorem:

$$P(\Theta, T) = p(\Theta|T)p(T) \tag{1}$$

where p(T) and $p(\Theta|T)$ show the prior distribution for the tree and parameters in terminal nodes given the tree, respectively. In this approach, a similar tree-generating stochastic process is used for p(T) of both classification and regression tree models [89], and this recursive stochastic process for tree growth includes the following steps:

- Start from T that includes only a root node (terminal node η).
- Slit terminal node η with probability $P_{SPLIT} = \alpha(1 + d_\eta)^{-\beta}$ (d_η shows the depth of the node η. α parameter is the base probability of tree growth by splitting a current node, and β parameter determines the rate at which the propensity to split decreases as the tree gets larger). α and β parameters control the shape and size of the tree and these parameters provide a penalty to avoid overfitting tree.
- If terminal node η splits, then a splitting rule ρ is assigned to this node according to the distribution P_{RULE} (discrete uniform distribution is used for selecting predictor variable to split the terminal node η and splitting threshold for this selected variable)
- Let T as newly created tree from step 3 and run steps 2 and 3 on this tree with η equal to the newly created child nodes.

In this approach, the posterior distribution function p(T|X, y) is computed with combining the marginal likelihood function p(Y|X, T) and tree prior p(T) as follows:

$$p(T|X, y) \propto p(y|X, T)\, p(T) \tag{2}$$

$$p(y|X, T) = \int p(y|X, \Theta, T)\, p(\Theta|T) d\Theta \tag{3}$$

$p(y|X, \Theta, T)$ in Eq. (3) shows the data likelihood function.

A stochastic search algorithm is used for finding good models and simulating from relation (2) by using a MCMC algorithm such as Metropolis-Hastings algorithm. This Metropolis-Hastings algorithm simulates a Markov chain sequence of trees namely $T^0, T^1, T^2, \ldots$, and this algorithm starts with an initial tree T^0, then iteratively simulates the transitions from T^i to T^{i+1} by two steps as shown below:

1. Generate a candidate value T^* with probability distribution $q(T^i, T^*)$.

2. Set $T^{i+1} = T^*$ with probability below:

$$\alpha(T^i, T^*) = \min\left\{\frac{q(T^*, T^i)\, p(Y|X, T^*)p(T^*)}{q(T^i, T^*)\, p(Y|X, T^i)p(T^i)}, 1\right\} \tag{4}$$

Else, set $T^{i+1} = T^i$.

In this simulation algorithm, $q(T, T^*)$ generates T^* from T by randomly selecting among four steps. These steps are GROW step, PRUNE step, CHANGE step, and SWAP step. This simulation algorithm is run with multiple restarts instead of a single long chain for reasons such as convergence of the posterior distribution or simulation chain, to avoid wasting long time waiting in areas of trees with high posterior distribution function, and generate a wide variety of different trees. Also, the stopping criterion of simulation algorithm is based on that the chain became trapped in a local posterior model.

This Bayesian approach unlike classic CART model does not generate a single tree, thus good trees for classification tree are selected based on criteria such as having lowest misclassification and largest marginal likelihood function. Also, good trees for regression tree are determined based on having the largest marginal likelihood function and lowest residual sums of squares. CGM by using simulation showed that stochastic search algorithm can find better trees than a greedy tree algorithm. They indicated that the Bayesian classification approach has lower misclassification rate than CART model and they also used Bayesian model averaging for improving prediction accuracy of Bayesian classification trees [89].

6.3 DMS'S Bayesian CART approach

DMS (Denison, Mallick, Smith) in 1998 proposed a Bayesian approach for the CART model, and this approach is quite similar to Bayesian approach of CGM with just minor differences [88]. In this approach, prior distributions are defined over the splitting node (S), splitting variable (V), splitting rule (R), tree size ($\mathcal{K}$), and parameters of data distribution in terminal nodes (ψ).

In this Bayesian approach, joint distribution of model parameters is defined as follows ($p(\mathcal{K})$: prior distribution for size of tree, $p(\theta_k|\mathcal{K})$: prior distribution for parameter set $\theta_k = \{R_k, S_k, V_k, \psi_k\}$ given $\mathcal{K}$ (tree size), $p(y|\mathcal{K}, \theta_k)$: data likelihood function):

$$p(\mathcal{K}, \theta_k, y) = p(\mathcal{K})\, p(\theta_k|\mathcal{K})\, p(y|\mathcal{K}, \theta_k) \tag{5}$$

This Bayesian approach puts a prior distribution over the tree size to avoid overfitting data and uses a truncated Poisson distribution with parameter λ (λ shows the expected number of nodes in the tree and a weakly informative is used prior for tree size by setting λ equal to 10) for $p(\mathcal{K})$ as follows:

$$p(\mathcal{K}) \propto \frac{\lambda^{\mathcal{K}}}{(e^{\lambda} - 1)\mathcal{K}!} \tag{6}$$

Also, $p(\theta_k|\mathcal{K})$ in Eq. (5) is defined as follows:

$$p(\theta_k|\mathcal{K}) = p(R_k|V_k, S_k, \mathcal{K})p(V_k|S_k, \mathcal{K})\, p(S_k|\mathcal{K})\, p(\psi_k|V, S, \mathcal{K}) \tag{7}$$

So, prior for this Bayesian approach is defined as follows:

$$p(\theta_k|\mathcal{K})\ p(\mathcal{K}) = p(R_k|V_k, S_k, \mathcal{K})p(V_k|S_k, \mathcal{K}) \\ p(S_k|\mathcal{K})\ p(\psi_k|V, S, \mathcal{K})\ p(\mathcal{K}) \tag{8}$$

In this approach, Bayesian analysis of tree size $\mathcal{K}$ and parameter set θ_k is as follows:

$$p(\theta_k, \mathcal{K}|y) = p(\mathcal{K}|y)\ p(\theta_k|\mathcal{K}, y) \tag{9}$$

Also, simulation from the above equation is done by using MCMC algorithms to find good trees and Reversible Jump MCMC algorithm is used to simulate from this equation [100]. This simulation algorithm is performed for a single long chain with a burn-in period to explore the tree space. In this simulation algorithm, trees cannot have sample size less than 5 in the terminal nodes and also cannot have size higher than 6 in during burn-in period of simulation chain of posterior distribution. Reversible Jump MCMC algorithm used by DMS to simulate from Eq. (9) includes four steps: BIRTH (GROW), DEATH (PRUNE), VARIABLE, and SPLITTING RULE. In this simulation algorithm, BIRTH step, DEATH step, VARIABLE step, and Splitting RULE step are randomly chosen with probability $b_{\mathcal{K}}$, $d_{\mathcal{K}}$, $V_{\mathcal{K}}$, and $R_{\mathcal{K}}$, respectively, and algorithm is as follows:

1. Stating with an initial tree.

2. Set $\mathcal{K}$ to the tree size in the present tree.

3. Generate $u \sim U[0, 1]$

4. Go to step type determined by u (a step type is determined based on following conditions):
   if ($u \le B_{\mathcal{K}}$), then go to BIRTH step
   else if ($b_{\mathcal{K}} \le u \le b_{\mathcal{K}} + d_{\mathcal{K}}$), then go to DEATH step
   else if ($b_{\mathcal{K}} + d_{\mathcal{K}} \le u \le b_{\mathcal{K}} + d_{\mathcal{K}} + V_{\mathcal{K}}$), then go to VARIABLE step
   else, go to RULE step

Then, acceptance probability (α) of each step that changes tree ($\mathcal{K}, \theta$) to tree ($\mathcal{K}^*, \theta^*$) as follows ($\mathcal{K}_{\text{die}}$ shows the number of possible locations for a death in the current tree):

$$\text{BIRTH step:}\alpha = \min\left\{1, (\text{likelihood ratio}) \times \frac{(\mathcal{K}_{\text{die}} + 1)}{\mathcal{K}}\right\} \tag{10}$$

$$\text{DEATH step:}\alpha = \min\left\{1, (\text{likelihood ratio}) \times \frac{\mathcal{K}}{(\mathcal{K}_{\text{die}} + 1)}\right\} \tag{11}$$

$$\text{VARIABLE and RULE steps:}\alpha = \min\{1, (\text{likelihood ratio})\} \tag{12}$$

if ($u \le \alpha$), then proposed tree to accept, else reject.

The stopping criterion of the above simulation algorithm is based on the stability of the posterior distribution and it can be assessed by drawing a plot of iterations of chain against sampled parameter values. This Bayesian approach, unlike CART, does not produce a tree using stochastic search algorithm. Thus, good classification trees are selected based on criteria such as misclassification rate, deviance ($-2\log p(y|\mathcal{K}, \theta_k)$), and posterior probability, and good classification trees have lowest misclassification rate, deviance, and largest posterior probability. Also, good regression trees have largest posterior probability and lowest residual sum of squares. DMS indicated that Bayesian approach provides richer output and superior performance than classic CART model [88].

6.4 CGM's hierarchical priors for Bayesian regression tree shrinkage approach

CGM, 2000 proposed a Bayesian approach for regression tree with mean-shift model based on computational strategy of CGM's Bayesian approach in 1998. Unlike the Bayesian approach (1998), it can assume dependence of parameters in the terminal nodes. Indeed, hierarchical priors are used for these parameters and therefore shrunk trees are generated [90]. Hierarchical priors have some advantages such as: shrinkage is used in the stochastic search algorithm unlike proposed methods for tree shrinkage (because these methods use shrinkage after searching tree), fitting a larger tree to the dataset without overfitting and improve predictions. CGM by using simulation showed the superior performance of new Bayesian approach for regression tree with mean-shift model in comparison to Bayesian approach of CGM in 1998, CART model, and tree shrinkage methods of Hastie and Pregibon [90, 101].

6.5 WTW'S Bayesian CART approach

WTW (Wu, Tjelmeland, West), 2007 proposed a Bayesian approach for CART model based on the computational strategy of Bayesian approach of CGM (1998) [95]. In this approach, prior distributions define on the tree, splitting variables, splitting thresholds, and parameters in the terminal nodes. This Bayesian approach like approaches of CGM [89, 90, 92, 93] simulates from the posterior distribution by using the Metropolis-Hastings algorithm. The steps used in simulation algorithm of WTW include GROW step and PRUNE step, CHANGE step, SWAP step, and RESTRUCTURE (RADICAL) step (first three steps are similar to steps of simulation algorithm in Bayesian approaches of CGM). RESTRUCTURE step creates large changes in the structure of tree, but tree size is unchanged. There are some advantages by adding this step to simulation algorithm of posterior distribution such as: improving the convergence of the MCMC algorithm, elimination of the need for restarts of the simulation algorithm unlike Bayesian approaches of CGM, and large changes in the structure of tree without change in tree size.

In this approach, convergence diagnostics of simulation algorithm are based on plots such as: plots of iteration number against log posterior distribution, log marginal likelihood function, number of terminal nodes, and number of times that a particular predictor variable is shown as a splitting variable in the tree. WTW showed the superior performance of Bayesian approach in comparison to CART model and that the Bayesian approach had a lower misclassification rate than the CART model [95].

6.6 OML'S Bayesian CART approach

OML (O'Leary, Mengersen, Low Choy), 2008, proposed a Bayesian approach for CART model by extending the Bayesian approach of DMS. These two Bayesian approaches have differences such as the stopping rule of the simulation algorithm or convergence diagnostic plots, criteria for identifying good trees and prior distributions considered for parameters in the terminal nodes [88, 96, 98].

The stopping criterion of simulation chain in OML'S Bayesian classification trees approach has two steps. The first step includes the plot of iterations against accuracy measures (false and positive negative rate and misclassification rate), log posterior, log likelihood, and tree size. If these plots show stability in mentioned items, then in second step, structure of component trees (variables and splitting rules at each splitting node) examines in the set of good trees and if this structure was stabilized and/or the same trees were in this set, then convergence has occurred for this simulation chain; otherwise, iterations must be increased until convergence.

The set of good trees in this Bayesian classification tree approach is determined based on the accuracy measures computed from the confusion matrix of Fielding and Bell [102]. Good trees have lowest misclassification rate and false positive and negative rate (or using highest sensitivity and specificity instead of lowest false positive and negative rate) [96, 98, 103]. After convergence of simulation chain, two or three trees are selected as the best trees among set of good trees based on criteria such as modal structure of tree (same size tree with the same variables and splitting rules), lowest misclassification rate, false negative and positive rate and deviance, highest posterior probability and likelihood, using expert judgment and biological interpretability [96, 98, 103].

The stopping rule of simulation algorithm for regression tree like classification tree includes two steps. In the first step, plot of iterations are drawn against posterior probability, residual sum of squares, and deviance. If these abovementioned items are stable, then structure of component trees examines in the set of good trees and if this structure was stabilized, convergence has been occurred for this simulation chain. Also, set of good trees for regression tree is selected based on having the highest posterior probability and likelihood, lowest residual sum of squares, and deviance [98].

OML compared the Bayesian classification trees with the classic CART model on an ecological dataset and concluded that Bayesian approach has smaller false positive rate, misclassification rate, and deviance than CART model, while the CART model has lower false negative rate, but this model had higher false positive rate [96]. They, in 2008, indicated that this Bayesian approach had a lower false negative rate in comparison to Bayesian approach of DMS, but approach of DMS had a lower false positive rate and misclassification rate [96].

OML in 2009 compared predictive performance of random forests with the Bayesian classification trees on the three datasets and they concluded that the best tree selected with Bayesian classification trees has higher sensitivity and better accuracy in comparison to random forests. They expressed that the Bayesian approach may have better performance than random forests in determining important predictor variables in datasets with a large number of noise predictor variables. OML also indicated that the Bayesian classification tree approach unlike random forests is not biased toward assignment of observations to the largest class of outcome variable in predicting data [103].

OML and Hu in 2011 compared the performance of Bayesian classification trees with the CART of Breiman et al., and they concluded that the Bayesian approach has higher sensitivity and specificity in comparison to CART. They also investigated overfitting of the Bayesian approach by using cross-validation method, and this approach did not show any evidence of overfitting [98].

6.7 OMML'S expert elicitation for Bayesian classification tree approach

OMML (O'Leary, Mengersen, Murray, Low Choy), 2008, proposed a Bayesian classification tree approach based on the computational strategy of Bayesian classification tree approach of OML and by using informative priors [96, 97]. In this Bayesian approach, informative priors are used to define Dirichlet distributions for splitting node, splitting variable, and splitting rule as follows:

$$p(S_k|\mathcal{K}) = \mathrm{Dir}(S_k|\alpha_{S_1},\ldots,\alpha_{S_k}) \tag{13}$$

$$p(V_k|S_k,\mathcal{K}) = \mathrm{Dir}(V_k|\alpha_{V_1},\ldots,\alpha_{V_k}) \tag{14}$$

$$p(R_k|V_k,S_k,\mathcal{K}) = \mathrm{Dir}(R_k|\alpha_{R_1},\ldots,\alpha_{R_k}) \tag{15}$$

In Bayesian approach of OML, there was no prior information about splitting node, splitting variable, splitting rule, and hyperparameters in the Dirichlet distributions of above equations. So, these hyperparameters were set equal to 1 and uniform non-informative priors used for splitting node, splitting variable, and splitting rule [96, 98, 103]. In this new approach, an expert is subjected with three questions (ordering, grading, and weighting) about splitting node, splitting variable, splitting rule, and tree size for defining informative priors. Then, existing hyperparameters in the relations (13), (14) and (15) are determined by following the result of a question. Three questions are used for size of the tree to determine λ in relation (6). DMS and OML used a weakly informative prior for tree size by setting $\lambda = 10$ [88, 96, 98, 103]. But OMML unlike DMS and OML used an informative prior for size of the tree [96, 97].

O'Leary et al. in 2008 investigated sensitivity to the choice of the hyperparameters of informative priors for tree size, splitting nodes, splitting variables, and splitting rules in classification trees and they concluded that posterior distribution is relatively robust to these priors except for extreme choices of them [96, 97].

OMML by simulation indicated that the best tree of Bayesian classification trees based on the informative priors has lower false negative rate in comparison to the best tree of Bayesian classification trees based on the non-informative priors [96, 97]. They also indicated the superior performance of Bayesian classification trees based on the informative priors in comparison to proposed expert elicitation approaches for Bayesian logistic regression model [97, 104–107].

6.8 Other approaches for Bayesian classification and regression trees

Pratola like Wu et al. proposed new Metropolis-Hastings proposals for Bayesian regression trees for improving the convergence of the MCMC algorithm [108]. CGM, 2003, proposed Bayesian treed GLMs by extending CGM's Bayesian approach (1998) [91]. Gramacy and Lee developed Bayesian treed Gaussian process models for a continuous outcome by combining standard Gaussian processes with treed partitioning [109]. Other Bayesian approaches are also proposed for tree-based models that we mention in the references. Refer to the Refs. [110–112] for other Bayesian tree approaches of CGM. Also, Chipman et al. review advance models for Bayesian treed methods and refer to the Ref. [113]. For study about other tree-based Bayesian approach, refer to Refs. [114–118]. Also, Refs. [119, 120] are proposed Bayesian approaches for ensemble trees.

7. Criteria for determining the predictive performance of classification and regression trees

Predictive performance of classification tree models can compare using accuracy measures such as [17, 121]: sensitivity, specificity, false positive rate, false negative rate, positive predictive value, negative predictive value, positive likelihood ratio, negative likelihood ratio, accuracy, Youden's index , diagnostic odds ratio (DOR), F-measure, and area under curve (AUC). Sensitivity, specificity, positive and negative predictive values, Youden's index, and accuracy have values between 0 and 1, and when these criteria are near to 1, then classification tree algorithm has better predictive performance. Also, false positive and false negative rates are between 0 and 1, and when these values are near to 0, then classification tree algorithm has better predictive performance. Classification tree models with positive likelihood ratio >10, negative likelihood ratio <0.1, and high diagnostic odds ratio have good predictive performance. AUC shows an overall performance measure and is between 0 and 1. Higher value shows an overall good performance measure, and a perfect diagnostic performance has an AUC equal to 1.

Predictive performance of regression tree algorithms can compare using criteria such as [122, 123]: Pearson correlation coefficient, root mean-squared error (RMSE), relative error (RE), mean error (ME), mean absolute errors (MAE), and bias.

8. Conclusion

Bayesian tree has some advantages in comparison to classic tree-based approaches. Classic CART model cannot explore the space of the tree fully and the result of tree is only locally optimal due to using greedy search algorithm. But Bayesian tree approaches investigate different tree structures with different splitting variables, splitting rules, and tree sizes, so these models can explore the tree space more than classic tree approaches. Indeed, Bayesian approaches are remedies for solving this problem of CART model. Also, CART is biased toward predictor variables with many distinct values, and Bayesian tree models can be a remedial for solving this problem. Because Bayesian approaches proposed by CGM, DMS, OML, and WTW utilize uniform distribution for selecting splitting node, splitting variables, and splitting rules, thus these approaches generate unbiased splits or have not any bias toward predictor variables with more splits. These approaches unlike classic tree approaches generate several trees that this advantage makes researchers to select the best tree based on study aim. Because in some studies, sensitivity is important for researcher and in other studies, specificity is important.

Some authors compared Bayesian approaches with classic tree approaches such as CART and random forests of Breiman and others models. Results of most papers indicated that Bayesian approach tends to present that the Bayesian method is superior to all other competitors. This can be for a variety of reasons: publication bias (methods that do not demonstrate superior performance typically do not get published), choice of examples that demonstrate superiority of their method, or more careful use of their method than the competing methods. Studies that may give more reliable comparisons would be ones in which there is no new method, and the paper is devoted to a comparison of existing approaches. For study about some of these papers, refer to Refs. [124–127].

According to empirical results, we can conclude that Bayesian approaches have better performance in comparison to classic CART model. Also, despite some advantages for Bayesian tree approaches in comparison with classic tree models, the number of published articles based on using Bayesian tree approaches for data analysis is low. One of the major reasons for this problem can be related to lack of user-friendly software and or need to have programming knowledge. On the other hand, the number of published papers based on employing CART model, random forests, and other classic tree models is many and one of the reasons for this frequency can be several software programs such as CART, SPSS, TANAGRA, STATISTICA, R, and WEKA.

Bayesian tree approaches need more research, because these approaches unlike CART and random forests cannot impute missing values. These approaches also cannot create linear combination splits like other tree algorithms (CART, QUEST, and CRUISE), even though interpretation of these splits is hard, but results indicated that tree methods with these splits have superior prediction accuracy in comparison to tree with univariate splits [128].

Author details

Amal Saki Malehi* and Mina Jahangiri
Faculty of Public Health, Department of Biostatistics and Epidemiology, Ahvaz Jundishapur University of Medical Sciences, Ahvaz, Iran

*Address all correspondence to: amalsaki@gmail.com

References

[1] Agresti A. Categorical Data Analysis. Hoboken, NJ: John Wiley & Sons; 2003

[2] Huberty CJ, Olejnik S. Applied MANOVA and Discriminant Analysis. Hoboken, NJ: John Wiley & Sons; 2006

[3] Klein JP, Moeschberger ML. Survival Analysis: Techniques for Censored and Truncated Data. New York: Springer Science & Business Media; 2006

[4] Moguerza JM, Muñoz A. Support vector machines with applications. Statistical Science. 2006;**21**(3):322-336

[5] Garson GD. Neural Networks: An Introductory Guide for Social Scientists. London: Sage; 1998

[6] Friedman JH, Roosen CB. An Introduction to Multivariate Adaptive Regression Splines. Thousand Oaks, CA: Sage Publications; 1995

[7] Duda RO, Hart PE, Stork DG. Pattern classification and scene analysis. New York: Wiley; 1973

[8] Friedman N, Geiger D, Goldszmidt M. Bayesian network classifiers. Machine Learning. 1997;**29**(2-3):131-163

[9] Hastie TJ. Generalized additive models. Statistical Models in S. Routledge; 2017. pp. 249-307

[10] De'ath G, Fabricius KE. Classification and regression trees: A powerful yet simple technique for ecological data analysis. Ecology. 2000;**81**(11):3178-3192

[11] Lemon SC, Roy J, Clark MA, Friedmann PD, Rakowski W. Classification and regression tree analysis in public health: Methodological review and comparison with logistic regression. Annals of Behavioral Medicine. 2003;**26**(3):172-181

[12] Speybroeck N, Berkvens D, Mfoukou-Ntsakala A, Aerts M, Hens N, Van Huylenbroeck G, et al. Classification trees versus multinomial models in the analysis of urban farming systems in Central Africa. Agricultural Systems. 2004;**80**(2):133-149

[13] Marshall RJ. The use of classification and regression trees in clinical epidemiology. Journal of Clinical Epidemiology. 2001;**54**(6):603-609

[14] Nelson LM, Bloch DA, Longstreth W, Shi H. Recursive partitioning for the identification of disease risk subgroups: A case-control study of subarachnoid hemorrhage. Journal of Clinical Epidemiology. 1998;**51**(3):199-209

[15] Camp NJ, Slattery ML. Classification tree analysis: A statistical tool to investigate risk factor interactions with an example for colon cancer (United States). Cancer Causes & Control. 2002;**13**(9):813-823

[16] El-Solh AA, Sikka P, Ramadan F. Outcome of older patients with severe pneumonia predicted by recursive partitioning. Journal of the American Geriatrics Society. 2001;**49**(12):1614-1621

[17] Jahangiri M, Khodadi E, Rahim F, Saki N, Saki Malehi A. Decision-tree-based methods for differential diagnosis of β-thalassemia trait from iron deficiency anemia. Expert Systems. 2017;**34**(3):e12201

[18] Loh WY, He X, Man M. A regression tree approach to identifying subgroups with differential treatment effects. Statistics in Medicine. 2015;**34**(11):1818-1833

[19] Li C, Glüer C-C, Eastell R, Felsenberg D, Reid DM, Roux C, et al. Tree-structured subgroup analysis of receiver operating characteristic

curves for diagnostic tests. Academic Radiology. 2012;**19**(12):1529-1536

[20] Zhang H, Singer BH. Recursive Partitioning and Applications. New York: Springer Science & Business Media; 2010

[21] Buntine W, Niblett T. A further comparison of splitting rules for decision-tree induction. Machine Learning. 1992;**8**(1):75-85

[22] De Mántaras RL. A distance-based attribute selection measure for decision tree induction. Machine Learning. 1991;**6**(1):81-92

[23] Friedman JH. A recursive partitioning decision rule for nonparametric classification. IEEE Transactions on Computers. 1977;**4**:404-408

[24] Rounds E. A combined nonparametric approach to feature selection and binary decision tree design. Pattern Recognition. 1980;**12**(5):313-317

[25] Ferri C, Flach P, Hernández-Orallo J, editors. Learning decision trees using the area under the ROC curve. ICML; 2002;**2**:139-146

[26] Mingers J. An empirical comparison of selection measures for decision-tree induction. Machine Learning. 1989;**3**(4):319-342

[27] Shih Y-S. Families of splitting criteria for classification trees. Statistics and Computing. 1999;**9**(4):309-315

[28] Quinlan JR. C4.5: Programs for Machine Learning. San Mateo, CA: Morgan Kaufmann; 1993

[29] Breiman L, Friedman J, Stone CJ, Olshen RA. Classification and Regression Trees. CRC press; 1984

[30] Kass GV. An exploratory technique for investigating large quantities of categorical data. Applied Statistics. 1980;**29**(2):119-127

[31] Loh W-Y, Vanichsetakul N. Tree-structured classification via generalized discriminant analysis. Journal of the American Statistical Association. 1988;**83**(403):715-725

[32] Loh W-Y, Shih Y-S. Split selection methods for classification trees. Statistica Sinica. 1997:815-840

[33] Kim H, Loh W-Y. Classification trees with unbiased multiway splits. Journal of the American Statistical Association. 2001;**96**(454):589-604

[34] Loh W-Y. Improving the precision of classification trees. The Annals of Applied Statistics. 2009;**3**(4):1710-1737

[35] Kim H, Loh W-Y. Classification trees with bivariate linear discriminant node models. Journal of Computational and Graphical Statistics. 2003;**12**(3):512-530

[36] Morgan JN, Sonquist JA. Problems in the analysis of survey data, and a proposal. Journal of the American Statistical Association. 1963;**58**(302):415-434

[37] Quinlan JR, editor. Learning with continuous classes. In: 5th Australian Joint Conference on Artificial Intelligence. World Scientific; 1992

[38] Loh W-Y. Regression tress with unbiased variable selection and interaction detection. Statistica Sinica. 2002;**12**:361-386

[39] Esposito F, Malerba D, Semeraro G, Kay J. A comparative analysis of methods for pruning decision trees. IEEE Transactions on Pattern Analysis and Machine Intelligence. 1997;**19**(5):476-491

[40] Mingers J. An empirical comparison of pruning methods for decision

tree induction. Machine Learning. 1989;**4**(2):227-243

[41] Quinlan JR, Rivest RL. Inferring decision trees using the minimum description lenght principle. Information and Computation. 1989;**80**(3):227-248

[42] Mehta M, Agrawal R, Rissanen J, editors. SLIQ: A fast scalable classifier for data mining. In: International Conference on Extending Database Technology. Springer; 1996

[43] Shafer J, Agrawal R, Mehta M, editors. SPRINT: A scalable parallel classi er for data mining. In: Proc 1996 Int Conf Very Large Data Bases. Citeseer; 1996

[44] Gehrke J, Ramakrishnan R, Ganti V. RainForest—A framework for fast decision tree construction of large datasets. Data Mining and Knowledge Discovery. 2000;**4**(2-3):127-162

[45] Murthy SK, Kasif S, Salzberg S. A system for induction of oblique decision trees. Journal of Artificial Intelligence Research. 1994;**2**:1-32

[46] Holte RC. Very simple classification rules perform well on most commonly used datasets. Machine Learning. 1993;**11**(1):63-90

[47] Müller W, Wysotzki F. Automatic construction of decision trees for classification. Annals of Operations Research. 1994;**52**(4):231-247

[48] Müller W, Wysotzki F. The decision-tree algorithm CAL5 based on a statistical approach to its splitting algorithm. Machine Learning and Statistics: The Interface. 1997. pp. 45-65

[49] Hothorn T, Hornik K, Zeileis A. Unbiased recursive partitioning: A conditional inference framework. Journal of Computational and Graphical Statistics. 2006;**15**(3):651-674

[50] Messenger R, Mandell L. A modal search technique for predictive nominal scale multivariate analysis. Journal of the American Statistical Association. 1972;**67**(340):768-772

[51] Biggs D, De Ville B, Suen E. A method of choosing multiway partitions for classification and decision trees. Journal of Applied Statistics. 1991;**18**(1):49-62

[52] Gray JB, Fan G. Classification tree analysis using TARGET. Computational Statistics and Data Analysis. 2008;**52**(3):1362-1372

[53] Quinlan JR. Induction of decision trees. Machine Learning. 1986;**1**(1):81-106

[54] Piccarreta R. Classification trees for ordinal variables. Computational Statistics. 2008;**23**(3):407-427

[55] Archer KJ. rpartOrdinal: An R package for deriving a classification tree for predicting an ordinal response. Journal of Statistical Software. 2010;**34**:7

[56] Galimberti G, Soffritti G, Maso MD. Classification trees for ordinal responses in R: The rpartScore package. Journal of Statistical Software. 2012;**47**(i10)

[57] Tutz G, Hechenbichler K. Aggregating classifiers with ordinal response structure. Journal of Statistical Computation and Simulation. 2005;**75**(5):391-408

[58] Kramer S, Widmer G, Pfahringer B, De Groeve M. Prediction of ordinal classes using regression trees. Fundamenta Informaticae. 2001;**47**(1-2):1-13

[59] Archer K, Mas V. Ordinal response prediction using bootstrap aggregation, with application to a high-throughput methylation data set. Statistics in Medicine. 2009;**28**(29):3597-3610

[60] Wheeler DC, Archer KJ, Burstyn I, Yu K, Stewart PA, Colt JS, et al. Comparison of ordinal and nominal classification trees to predict ordinal expert-based occupational exposure estimates in a case-control study. Annals of Occupational Hygiene. 2014;**59**(3):324-335

[61] Liu W, Chawla S, Cieslak DA, Chawla NV, editors. A robust decision tree algorithm for imbalanced data sets. In: Proceedings of the 2010 SIAM International Conference on Data Mining. SIAM; 2010

[62] Cieslak DA, Hoens TR, Chawla NV, Kegelmeyer WP. Hellinger distance decision trees are robust and skew-insensitive. Data Mining and Knowledge Discovery. 2012;**24**(1):136-158

[63] Ganganwar V. An overview of classification algorithms for imbalanced datasets. International Journal of Emerging Technology and Advanced Engineering. 2012;**2**(4):42-47

[64] Yang L, Liu S, Tsoka S, Papageorgiou LG. A regression tree approach using mathematical programming. Expert Systems with Applications. 2017;**78**:347-357

[65] Su X, Wang M, Fan J. Maximum likelihood regression trees. Journal of Computational and Graphical Statistics. 2004;**13**(3):586-598

[66] Choi Y, Ahn H, Chen JJ. Regression trees for analysis of count data with extra Poisson variation. Computational Statistics and Data Analysis. 2005;**49**(3):893-915

[67] Therneau TM, Atkinson EJ. An Introduction to Recursive Partitioning using the RPART Routines. Technical Report 61. 1997. Available from: http://www.mayo.edu/hsr/techrpt/61.pdf

[68] Loh W-Y. Regression tree models for designed experiments. Institute of Mathematical Statistics. 2006. pp. 210-228

[69] Lee S-K, Jin S. Decision tree approaches for zero-inflated count data. Journal of Applied Statistics. 2006;**33**(8):853-865

[70] Wang Y, Witten IH. Induction of Model Trees for Predicting Continuous Classes; 1996

[71] Chan K-Y, Loh W-Y. LOTUS: An algorithm for building accurate and comprehensible logistic regression trees. Journal of Computational and Graphical Statistics. 2004;**13**(4):826-852

[72] Zeileis A, Hothorn T, Hornik K. Model-based recursive partitioning. Journal of Computational and Graphical Statistics. 2008;**17**(2):492-514

[73] Chaudhuri P, Lo W-D, Loh W-Y, Yang C-C. Generalized regression trees. Statistica Sinica. 1995;**5**:641-666

[74] Chaudhuri P, Huang M-C, Loh W-Y, Yao R. Piecewise-polynomial regression trees. Statistica Sinica. 1994;**4**:143-167

[75] Alexander WP, Grimshaw SD. Treed regression. Journal of Computational and Graphical Statistics. 1996;**5**(2):156-175

[76] Karalič A, editor. Employing linear regression in regression tree leaves. In: Proceedings of the 10th European Conference on Artificial Intelligence. John Wiley & Sons, Inc; 1992

[77] Landwehr N, Hall M, Frank E. Logistic model trees. Machine Learning. 2005;**59**(1-2):161-205

[78] Grubinger T, Zeileis A, Pfeiffer KP. evtree: Evolutionary Learning of Globally Optimal Classification and Regression Trees in R. Working Papers in Economics and Statistics; 2011

[79] Breiman L. Statistical modeling: The two cultures (with comments and a rejoinder by the author). Statistical Science. 2001;**16**(3):199-231

[80] Loh WY. Tree-structured classifiers. Wiley Interdisciplinary Reviews: Computational Statistics. 2010;**2**(3):364-369

[81] Loh WY. Classification and regression trees. Wiley Interdisciplinary Reviews: Data Mining and Knowledge Discovery. 2011;**1**(1):14-23

[82] Breiman L. Random forests. Machine Learning. 2001;**45**(1):5-32

[83] Breiman L. Bagging predictors. Machine Learning. 1996;**24**(2):123-140

[84] Freund Y, Schapire RE. Experiments with a New Boosting Algorithm. ICML. 1996;**96**:148-156

[85] Webb GI. Multiboosting: A technique for combining boosting and wagging. Machine Learning. 2000;**40**(2):159-196

[86] Friedman J, Hastie T, Tibshirani R. Additive logistic regression: A statistical view of boosting (with discussion and a rejoinder by the authors). The Annals of Statistics. 2000;**28**(2):337-407

[87] Buntine W. Learning classification trees. Statistics and Computing. 1992;**2**(2):63-73

[88] Denison DG, Mallick BK, Smith AF. A bayesian CART algorithm. Biometrika. 1998;**85**(2):363-377

[89] Chipman HA, George EI, McCulloch RE. Bayesian CART model search. Journal of the American Statistical Association. 1998;**93**(443):935-948

[90] Chipman H, McCulloch RE. Hierarchical priors for Bayesian CART shrinkage. Statistics and Computing. 2000;**10**(1):17-24

[91] Chipman H, George E, McCulloch R. Bayesian treed generalized linear models. Bayesian Statistics. 2003;**7**:323-349

[92] Chipman HA, George EI, McCulloch RE. Bayesian treed models. Machine Learning. 2002;**48**(1-3):299-320

[93] Moe WW, Chipman H, George EI, McCulloch RE. A Bayesian Treed Model of Online Purchasing Behavior Using in-Store Navigational Clickstream. Revising for 2nd Review at Journal of Marketing Research; 2002

[94] Pittman J, Huang E, Nevins J, Wang Q, West M. Bayesian analysis of binary prediction tree models for retrospectively sampled outcomes. Biostatistics. 2004;**5**(4):587-601

[95] Wu Y, Tjelmeland H, West M. Bayesian CART: Prior specification and posterior simulation. Journal of Computational and Graphical Statistics. 2007;**16**(1):44-66

[96] O'Leary RA. Informed Statistical Modelling of Habitat Suitability for Rare and Threatened Species (Doctoral dissertation, Queensland University of Technology). 2008

[97] O'Leary RA, Murray JV, Low Choy SJ, Mengersen KL. Expert elicitation for Bayesian classification trees. Journal of Applied Probability and Statistics. 2008;**3**(1):95-106

[98] Hu W, O'Leary RA, Mengersen K, Choy SL. Bayesian classification and regression trees for predicting incidence of cryptosporidiosis. PLoS One. 2011;**6**(8):e23903

[99] Quinlan JR, Compton PJ, Horn K, Lazarus L, editors. Inductive knowledge acquisition: A case study. In: Proceedings of the Second Australian

Conference on Applications of Expert Systems. Addison-Wesley Longman Publishing Co., Inc; 1987

[100] Green PJ. Reversible jump Markov chain Monte Carlo computation and Bayesian model determination. Biometrika. 1995;**82**(4):711-732

[101] Hastie T, Pregibon D. Shrinking trees. AT & T Bell Laboratories Technical Report; 1990

[102] Fielding AH, Bell JF. A review of methods for the assessment of prediction errors in conservation presence/absence models. Environmental Conservation. 1997;**24**(01):38-49

[103] O'Leary R, Francis R, Carter K, Firth M, Kees U, de Klerk N. A Comparison of Bayesian Classification Trees and Random Forest to Identify Classifiers for Childhood Leukaemia. Proc. 18th World IMACS Congr. Int. Congr. Modell. Simul. Modell. Simul. Soc. Aust. NZ Int. Assoc. Math. Comput. Simul.(MODSIM09). 2009:4276-4282

[104] O'Leary RA, Choy SL, Murray JV, Kynn M, Denham R, Martin TG, et al. Comparison of three expert elicitation methods for logistic regression on predicting the presence of the threatened brush-tailed rock-wallaby *Petrogale penicillata*. Environmetrics. 2009;**20**(4):379-398

[105] Kynn M. Eliciting Expert Knowledge for Bayesian Logistic Regression in Species Habitat Modelling; 2005

[106] Denham R, Mengersen K. Geographically assisted expert elicitation for species' distribution models. Bayesian Analysis. 2007;**2**(1):99-136

[107] O'Leary R, Mengersen K, Murray J, Low Choy S, editors. Comparison of four expert elicitation methods: For Bayesian logistic regression and classification trees. In: 18th World Imacs Congress and Modsim09 International Congress on Modelling and Simulation. Modelling and Simulation Society of Australia and New Zealand; 2009

[108] Pratola MT. Efficient Metropolis-Hastings proposal mechanisms for Bayesian regression tree models. Bayesian Analysis. 2016;**11**(3):885-911

[109] Gramacy RB, Lee HKH. Bayesian treed Gaussian process models with an application to computer modeling. Journal of the American Statistical Association. 2008;**103**(483):1119-1130

[110] Chipman HA, George EI, McCulloch RE. Bayesian ensemble learning. Advances in Neural Information Processing Systems. 2007;**19**:265

[111] Chipman HA, George EI, McCulloch RE. BART: Bayesian additive regression trees. The Annals of Applied Statistics. 2010;**4**:266-298

[112] Pratola MT, Chipman HA, Gattiker JR, Higdon DM, McCulloch R, Rust WN. Parallel Bayesian additive regression trees. Journal of Computational and Graphical Statistics. 2014;**23**(3):830-852

[113] Chipman H, George EI, Gramacy RB, McCulloch R. Bayesian treed response surface models. Wiley Interdisciplinary Reviews: Data Mining and Knowledge Discovery. 2013;**3**(4):298-305

[114] Angelopoulos N, Cussens J, editors. Tempering for Bayesian C&RT. In: Proceedings of the 22nd International Conference on Machine Learning. ACM; 2005

[115] Schetinin V, Fieldsend JE, Partridge D, Krzanowski WJ, Everson RM, Bailey TC, et al. The Bayesian Decision Tree

Technique with A Sweeping Strategy. arXiv preprint cs/0504042; 2005

[116] Lakshminarayanan B, Roy D, Teh YW, editors. Top-down particle filtering for Bayesian decision trees. In: International Conference on Machine Learning. 2013

[117] Lakshminarayanan B, Roy D, Teh YW, editors. Particle Gibbs for Bayesian additive regression trees. In: Artificial Intelligence and Statistics. 2015

[118] Taddy MA, Gramacy RB, Polson NG. Dynamic trees for learning and design. Journal of the American Statistical Association. 2011;**106**(493):109-123

[119] Duan LL, Clancy JP, Szczesniak RD. Bayesian ensemble trees (BET) for clustering and prediction in heterogeneous data. Journal of Computational and Graphical Statistics. 2016;**25**(3):748-761

[120] Quadrianto N, Ghahramani Z. A very simple safe-Bayesian random forest. IEEE Transactions on Pattern Analysis and Machine Intelligence. 2015;**37**(6):1297-1303

[121] Šimundić A-M. Measures of diagnostic accuracy: Basic definitions. Medical and biological Sciences. 2008;**22**(4):61-65

[122] Etemad-Shahidi A, Mahjoobi J. Comparison between M5′ model tree and neural networks for prediction of significant wave height in Lake Superior. Ocean Engineering. 2009;**36**(15-16):1175-1181

[123] Taghizadeh-Mehrjardi R, Dehghani S, Sahebjalal E. Comparison of multiple linear regression and regression tree for prediction of saturated hydraulic conductivity and macroscopic capillary length (Î±*). ProEnvironment/ ProMediu. 2013;**6**(13)

[124] Chen M, Cho J, Zhao H. Detecting epistatic SNPs associated with complex diseases via a Bayesian classification tree search method. Annals of Human Genetics. 2011;**75**(1):112-121

[125] Freeman AM, Lamon EC, Stow CA. Nutrient criteria for lakes, ponds, and reservoirs: A Bayesian TREED model approach. Ecological Modelling. 2009;**220**(5):630-639

[126] Lamon EC, Malve O, Pietiläinen O-P. Lake classification to enhance prediction of eutrophication endpoints in Finnish lakes. Environmental Modelling and Software. 2008;**23**(7):938-947

[127] Lamon EC, Stow CA. Bayesian methods for regional-scale eutrophication models. Water Research. 2004;**38**(11):2764-2774

[128] Lim T-S, Loh W-Y, Shih Y-S. A comparison of prediction accuracy, complexity, and training time of thirty-three old and new classification algorithms. Machine Learning. 2000;**40**(3):203-228

Chapter 4

Automatic Mapping of Student 3D Profiles in Software Metrics for Temporal Analysis of Programming Learning and Scoring Rubrics

Márcia Gonçalves de Oliveira, Ádler Oliveira Silva Neves and Mônica Ferreira Silva Lopes

Abstract

The purpose of this chapter is to present an online system for a 3D representation of programming students' profiles on software metrics that quantify effort and quality of programming from the analysis of source codes. In this representation, each student profile is a three-dimensional vector represented by a set of programming solutions developed by a student and mapped on 348 metrics of software during a programming course. Applying this profile representation, we developed a system with the following functionalities: generation of student's timelines to verify the evolution of metrics in a sequence of programming solutions over a course, different visualizations of these variables, automatic selection of representative codes for composition of rubrics with less effort of evaluation and selection of metrics that more influence in scores attributed by teachers. The advantages of this system are to enable the analysis of where the learning difficulties begin, the monitoring of how a class evolves along a course and the dynamic composition of rubric representations to inform assessment criteria. The system proposed therefore presents itself as a relevant tool to assist teachers about decisions of an evaluative process, allowing in fact to assist students from the beginning to the end of a course.

Keywords: learning analysis, programming, software metrics, learning profiles

1. Introduction

Analysis of programming learning for purposes of assisting and qualifying a learning process from beginning to end represents an onerous task to programming practice, since the practice of assisted programming spends time and effort in activities, assessment, especially when there is the application of a lot of exercises and there are many students in a class. Thus, applying learning analysis that makes it possible to compare programming solutions developed by different students and to verify how a student's solution evolve over time represent a real challenge for the evaluation of programming.

Although there are already several solutions for representing and comparing programming students' profiles [1, 2], there are few solutions for a temporal analysis of the learning of these students during a programming course.

A more recent proposal to analyze programming learning aims to map source codes into software metrics that quantify effort and quality of programming [3]. Through these metrics, for each programming activity, it is possible to compare student's solutions under different variables to identify classes of solutions, common learning difficulties, good practices of programming and even plagiarism.

Although the proposal of [3] makes it possible to compare student profiles of a class in each programming activity, it is laborious for a teacher through this instrument to verify how these evaluation metrics evolve over time, that is, to each activity of a course, for each student. This type of monitoring allows the programming teacher to identify in which students develop better in their learning processes and where students begin to present learning difficulties.

In order to meet this need by offering programming teachers an instrument to monitor the learning process of their students, this chapter extends the proposal of [3] generating 3D views of student profiles mapped into selected software metrics. These metrics characterize each student's efficiency, style, and programming effort with each programming solution they develop over a course.

In addition to the 3D representation to analyze learning, this system selects dynamically programming solution samples for a teacher to score until finding a representative set of rubric representations to inform evaluation criteria. This functionality may contribute later to generate a representative set of programs to train automatic assessment system of programming exercises.

Another feature of this system that is still in the testing phase is the prediction of students' performances in an activity based on their history of solving activities or the solutions of that same activity developed by other students.

The main contribution of this chapter is, therefore, offering a tool to support evaluation, decision-making in the field of programming, enabling teachers to analyze and monitor their students' learning for each programming activity under a wide range of variables, anticipating a predictable future of poor performance.

In order to present the fundamentals and the functionalities of the proposed system, this chapter is organized in the following order. Section 2 presents the related work. Section 3 describes the system architecture with 3D representations of profiles and the selection of rubric representations. Section 4 highlights reports of application of our system in a programming distance course. Section 5 concludes this work highlighting the main results, future work and final considerations.

2. Static analysis of programming

Static analysis is an automatic assessment approach to programming learning based on analysis of code. Through static analysis, it is possible to analyze effort, complexity, efficiency and quality of programming [4–6].

The main advantages of static analysis are lower cost, less reliance on the teacher's reference solution and the possibility of offering an evaluation closer to human evolution, although many programming teachers have prioritize the dynamic analysis, which is an analysis based on the correct and efficient execution of programs. Static analysis can therefore be used in the analysis of programming codes for the following purposes:

- Effort measurement and coding complexity [4]
- Prediction of performance [7, 8]
- Programming style analysis [5, 9]
- Evaluation by software metrics [3, 10]
- Recognition of signs of plagiarism [3]
- Recognition of rubrics [11]
- Recommendation of activities [1]
- Programming proficiency analysis [12]
- Analysis of learning difficulties and good programming practices [3].

Among the technological solutions of programming learning analysis based on static analysis already proposed, we highlight: the metrics of Halstead and McCabe [4, 5, 13], the evaluation of programming skills by software metrics [10], the recommendation system of activities according to learning difficulties [1], the analysis of difficulties by software metrics [3], the evaluation of how programming students learn from the analysis of their programming codes [14] and the programming proficiency analysis of SCALE system [12].

2.1 The evolution of static analysis strategies of programming

The main static analysis strategies of programming developed from the 1960s to the present day were based on software evaluation metrics that evolved from the purposes of measuring codes and software quality for educational purposes of diagnosing learning difficulties and evaluating difficulties, skills and even programming skills.

In the 1970s and 1980s, the software metrics were used to analyze programming codes for the purposes of estimating effort, complexity and programming style. Thus, some developed strategies were associated the programming process with the psychological complexity to evaluate performance in programming without necessarily having the concern to help those who had more difficulties [4, 9].

During the 90s until the year 2010, strategies of static analysis based on metrics for learning analysis, but in times when the Intelligent Tutoring Systems (ITS) were high, it was sought to represent the model or profile of a student, focusing more on his learning.

In more recent research on programming learning analysis, in addition to having a concern to better understand the students' learning profiles, there have been attempts to remedy learning difficulties [3]. Other trends in programming learning analysis are proficiency assessment [12], prediction of performances [15] and the classification of profiles by learning levels [2].

2.2 Related works

The main related works to our proposal are the assessment system based on the software metrics of [3], the instruments of visualization of programming students' profiles of [16], the recognition strategy of profiles by source code analysis metrics of [2], the selection model of features of [17], the system of recognition of rubrics with dimensionality reduction of [11] and the study of [18] involving the discovery of longitudinal patterns.

PCodigo II is an online system of automatic mapping of students' profiles in software metrics to analyze programming learning [3]. In addition to profiling mapping in 348 software metrics, PCodigo II has massive execution, similar profile graphing, information visualization, and plagiarism analysis capabilities.

The first applications of PCodigo II of [3] in real programming exercises demonstrate the effectiveness of this system for the diagnostic assessment of programming learning. Thus applying PCodigo II in real programming exercises it was shown that teachers, taking into account what the metrics say, can recognize the learning difficulties, good programming practices and classes of learning profiles of a whole class in a fast, detailed and holistic way.

The chapter of [16] presents some information visualization instruments in a multidimensional perspective to help teachers in the analysis of programming learning with mapping of profiles on software metrics. Through generated visualizations, we can analyze and compare profiles under different variables to recognize learning difficulties and classes of solutions from similar characteristics.

The strategy of profile recognition by static analysis of codes based on metrics of [2] aims to infer profiles of programmers from analysis of their Java code, classify them according to skills and continually evaluate their progress in the practice of programming in a course. The detected profiles are a novice, advanced beginner, proficient and expert.

Some metrics used in this strategy are a number of sentences, conditional control and repetition structures, types of data, classes, operators, lines of code, and other code. The advantage of this strategy in relation to our system is to classify and qualify students. However, we automatically select the most appropriate metrics to evaluate each type of programming solution.

For an automatic selection of evaluation variables, we highlight the selection model of the characteristics of [17], which combines clustering techniques and algorithm to create a feature map by selecting relevant terms in the texts of the groups of notes of the evaluation of a teacher. In our proposal, the relevant characteristics, that is, the most important metrics for each programming solution, we can visualize through heat maps comparing different solutions from five or more software metrics.

Regarding the composition of rubrics, a strategy to highlight is the proposal of [11], which is based on clustering and Principal Component Analysis techniques to recognize, from solutions developed by students, examples of solutions that represent, in a rubric scheme, the scores attributed by a teacher. This work complements these proposals by generating a ranking of samples of programming solutions for a teacher to score until finding the best set of rubric representations with a diversity of marks awarded.

According to [18], to understand how learning unfolds in the over time, it is necessary to move to a new learning perspective in which the units of analysis are separate but interrelated learning events.

Following this idea, the study of [18] investigates and validates longitudinal patterns in online participation as a measure to differentiate student performances.

The proposal of the system of this work, based on the study of [18], seeks to understand how programming learning unfolds and analyze longitudinal patterns.

In this way, following this proposal, in relation to the other Works Presented, we advanced in the 3D representation of profiles of programming students, in the view of characteristics represented by software metrics over time and the composition of rubrics from a ranking of selected solutions automatically for a teacher to score.

3. 3D representation system of programming students' profiles

The system of representation of profiles presented in this chapter is an evolution of *PCodigo II*, a software developed by which, by software metrics that quantifies effort and quality of programming, recognizes possible learning difficulties, good programming practices and until strong evidence of plagiarism among programs [3].

Thus our system extends the students' profiles representation of *PCodigo II* in a temporal dimension, selects more relevant metrics and allows the automatic selection of representative examples from a set of source codes for composition of rubric representation.

Figure 1 shows the system's architecture proposed in a scheme of inputs, processing and outputs come an integration of our system to the 1.0 and 3. x versions of *Moodle* virtual learning environment.

According to **Figure 1**, for version 1.9 of *Moodle*, the system receives as input a backup of Moodle's *Compacted Classroom* (in .zip, .rar, .gz or .tgz formats). For version 3. x of *Moodle*, the system is accessed through *Teacher's Credentials* to access a distance programming course of *Moodle*.

The course data imported from *Moodle* are as follows: student listing, activity listing, activity notes and *Submissions*, that are files of programming exercises. These data are then extracted by the *Extracting and Preprocessing* module and *Submissions* containing source codes that were written in C, C++, Java or Python languages are mapped to vectors whose dimensions are software metrics that quantify effort and quality of programming [3]. The submitted C programs are mapped on 348 software metrics and the Python programs, in 42 metrics.

Each vector representation on software metrics of a student's programming solution we call *Learning State*. Then, after generating *Learning States* of a programming class, the system gathers these representations in a *Cognitive Matrix* for analysis and comparison of programs written by students [3].

In order to analyze solutions in a generic way, we have reduced each *Learning State* to five metrics: *Maintainability*, *Cyclomatic Complexity*, *Indentation*, *Laconism* and *Modularization*. They are described as follows:

- *Maintainability* represents the student's ability to write durable and adaptable code to new needs.

- *Cyclomatic Complexity* informs the complexity of a programming code that is the number of paths of a method [Curtis et al. 1979].

- *Indentation metric* characterizes the instructions of a program within structures and functions.

- *Laconism* expresses the capacity to express itself in a few words that in programming is measured by the number of tokens per line of code.

- *Modularization* informs organizational capacity of the parts of a functional or data module.

Then, bringing together the cognitive matrices for each programming solution of a course, a *3D Representation of Learning Profiles* of a programming class. The same procedure is performed for a *Reduced Matrix*. This timeline formed by a set of *Learning States* of a student over a course is called *Learning Profile*.

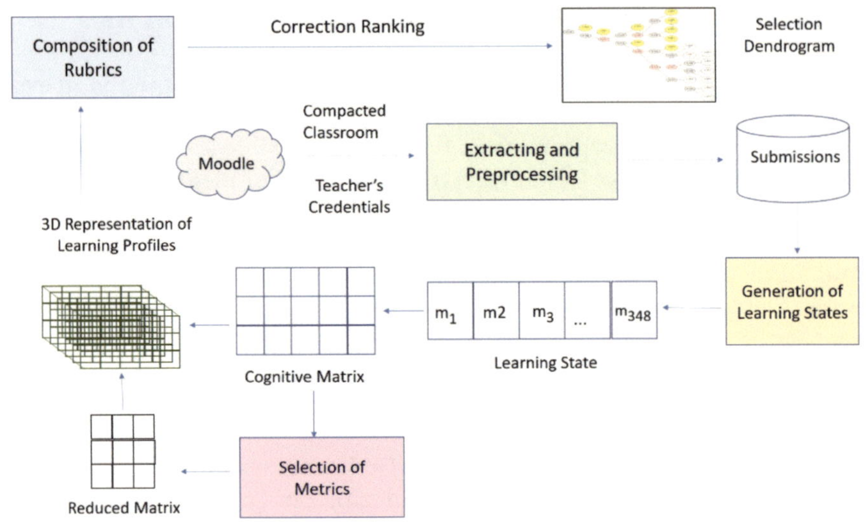

Figure 1.
Architecture of the 3D representation system of students' profiles.

Learning Profile shows how a set of student's assessment variables evolves over a course. Thus, through the analysis of profiles of learning it is possible to understand main learning difficulties of students and to reorient teaching with formative assessment actions in order to anticipate the predictable future of poor performances.

3.1 Selection of metrics

The Reduced Matrix generation process is performed by *Selection of Metrics* module (see **Figure 1**) using the *Recursive Feature Elimination* (RFE) method of the *Scikit-Learn* library [19] and a linear regression algorithm. The inputs of *Selection of Metrics* are the grades of some programming solutions and the *Cognitive Matrix* mapped on 348 software metrics generated by *PCodigo II* [3]. The *Selection of Metrics* returns the metrics most related to the grading pattern through a metric ranking.

3.2 Timeline of programming solutions

The timeline consists of a vector representation of the five fundamental metrics or selected metrics most closely related to a teacher's grade from each course programming exercise. This representation contributes to the analysis of how the evaluation metrics evolve for each student during a course and to generate a training set from to predict future exercise performance from history of exercises and performances associated with them.

3.3 Clusters analysis and composition of rubrics

A hierarchical approach we have used s to form clusters of similar solutions. In this way, a representative would be selected from each of these clusters to receive a teacher's grade and that grade would be reproduced for the other standards in the same cluster.

Unlike PCodigo II [3], in which clustering is performed with a previously defined number of clusters, a dendrogram based on centroid was generated, from which can be extracted the amount of clusters required, which, in this work, was placed as half of the samples from the algorithm BFS (*Breadth-first search*) tree, where the depth is given by the distance noted on each edge, that is *Euclidean Distance.*

According to **Figure 1**, for *Composition of Rubrics* with the purpose of assisting teacher's programming exercises, we have developed an automatic selection of representative samples of codes and metrics more related to the marks assigned by a teacher to this small set of representative codes.

In order to select this small set of representative codes, we have used a hierarchical representation of clusters by *Selection Dendrogram* with Euclidean Distance similarity measure. In *Selection Dendrogram*, the first samples marked yellow are the samples selected from *Correction Ranking,* that is a list automatically generated to indicate the best correction sequence of programming exercises so that the teacher can score a smaller set of samples of programs that represents the diversity of marks.

Through this representation, a search in depth not aware of plagiarism is performed starting with the more atypical samples and accumulating distances (from root to node) which are expressed at each node of the dendrogram. Then, after the selected samples are scored by a teacher and the metrics that most impact the grades assigned by him are verified to analyze possible correction inconsistencies.

3.4 Prediction of performance

In order to begin the performance prediction experiments, we have chosen two prediction methods: based on cluster analysis and based on previous performance histories.

In prediction based on cluster analysis, we used the selection ranking that selects representative samples of the *Dendrogram Selection* subgraphs to form a training set of the prediction model based on linear regression with 50% examples of a set of punctuated programming solutions by a teacher. The other 50% are predicted automatically by prediction model with reference based on diversity of the scores assigned by a teacher to the training set examples.

In the prediction of performances based on a history of previous performances, through a time series generated from the 3D representation (students × activities × metrics), a regressor model of each metric is trained and a regressor of metrics for grades, then the metrics of the next exercise are predicted as well as your grade. In this case, the training set is represented by the solutions solved by the same student along the course and the note to be predicted is the next solution to the history samples of that set.

4. Experiments and results

The first experiments of the system functionalities proposed in this chapter were in a Moodle's classroom of a distance course of C Programming Language in Brazil. Through the access credentials of a programming teacher, we obtained a zipped copy of the classroom from this course to the processing of learning analysis from students' codes. Next, all C programming code files were extracted along the programming distance course by about 25 programming students.

After the generation of 3D representations of learning profiles (*Activities* × *Students* × *Metrics*), gathering 10 activities, 25 students and 348 metrics of software, we use this information to generate the following results and views:

- For each activity, the list of metrics that were considered the most relevant to assign marks.

- For a class as a whole, a list of selected metrics from 348 metrics, that were considered the most relevant to assign marks.
- Dendrogram automatically generated on all the metrics that make up the student profile.
- Dendrogram automatically generated on all the metrics that make up the student profile, after normalization to values between 0 and 1.
- A heat map for each activity with selected metrics that best represent each activity.
- A heat map for each activity with the metrics that best represent the marking criterion for the class as a whole.
- A heat map for each student (historical in time) with the metrics that best represent the correction criterion for the class as a whole.
- A heat map for each activity with five metrics representing skills and difficulties programming.
- A heat map for each student (historical in time) with five metrics representing the students' programming skills and difficulties.
- Prediction of student grades, where grades are assigned to submissions that are similar to each other.

One of the activities we use for this experiment was applied in a C programming distance course and contains the following statement:

Write a program to get the number of P points of three teams in a football championship, according to the following mathematical expression:

$$P = 5GP - GN + 3VF + 2VC + E$$

In this formula, GP is the number of positive goals, GN is the number of goals taken, VF is the number of wins away from home, VC is the number of victories at home and E is the number of draws. The output of this program must show, according to the number of points obtained by a team, the champion and the runner-up of a championship.

We chose this activity for learning analysis because the use of logical expressions and conditional and repetitive control structures allows us to differentiate the solutions in order to recognize which solutions show difficulties to construct logical expressions in control structures. In this way, a good solution of this activity will present few comparisons and a few lines of programming code. On the other hand, a solution with several comparisons, instructions and control structures built into the arrangement evidences programming effort and difficulties to construct logical sentences.

In **Figure 2**, using this activity as an example of results 1 and 2, and views 5, 6, we highlight two modes of analysis of programming solutions of our system for a programming activity: first, from software metrics *Maintainability, Cyclomatic Complexity*, *Indentation*, *Laconism* and *Modularization and from* metrics that were considered the most relevant for the attribution of marks, that is, the *Reduced Matrix* metrics.

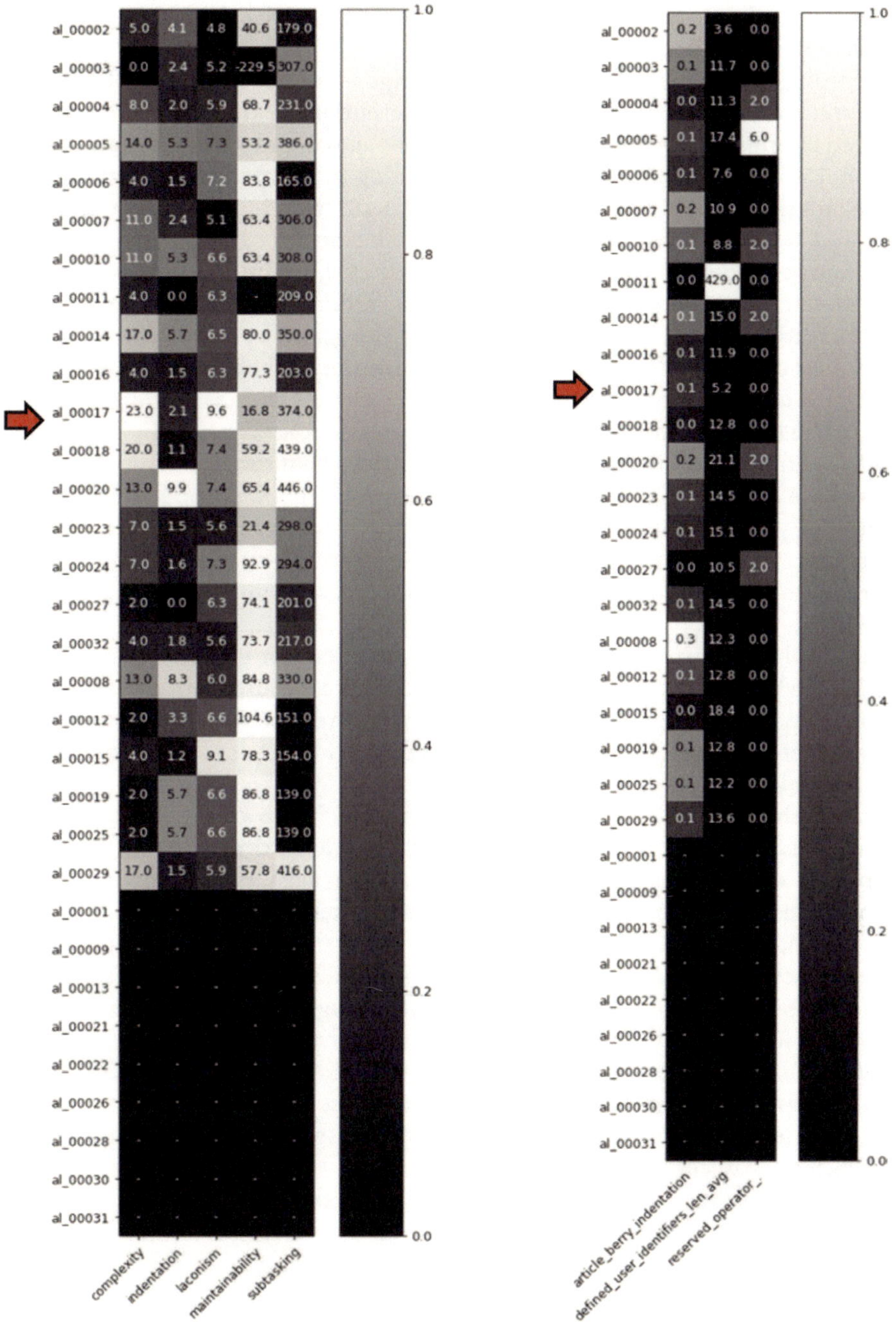

Figure 2.
Analysis of solutions by software metrics.

In graphs of **Figure 2**, the columns indicate students' solutions and columns, metrics. In each column, the white color (scale 1) indicates the highest value and the black color (scale 0), the smallest value of a metric. The interpretation of whether the higher value is better depends on the level of information of each code. However, the teacher can perform this interpretation comparing value of the best solutions and the worst solution. In this way, it would have an instrument to evaluate which indicators characterize good programming solutions and those that express the most difficulties.

According to **Figure 2**, in the first graph, high value of *Complexity*, low value of *Indentation* and high value of *Laconism* differentiate *al_00017 solution*, that is indicated by the red arrow in **Figure 2**, from too much and stand out as a poor solution. In the second graph, however, according to the assessment criteria based on three metrics related to a teacher's mark, this solution follows the pattern of the others and is therefore not indicated as a bad solution.

In **Figure 3**, where there is an example of view 9, we highlight how the five major metrics evolve each exercise for a same student over a course. It is observed that this student, indicated in the first line of the graph by a green arrow, has a predominance of the black color in his programming solution, indicating low values, and meaning good performances in the easiest exercises. On the other hand, in the last exercise by a red arrow he did, the colors appear lighter, indicating more complex activities and more difficulties. That more evident when, from this exercise that has higher *Complexity* value, the student stopped delivering the activities of programming, as it is noticed in the black color indicating a lack of performance in the following activities. We see in this visualization the potential of the tool to enable a teacher to recognize where a student began to demonstrate difficulties.

The graph of **Figure 4** is the ranking view for a teacher to assign marks to activities with the least effort of correcting. This graph is a dendrogram that presents the hierarchy of developed solutions for a programming activity represented by software metrics normalized to values between 0 and 1. Distances are marked in gray and pink.

The graph of **Figure 5** is a ranking view for a teacher to assign marks to activities with the least effort of correcting. This graph is a dendrogram that presents the hierarchy of developed solutions for a programming activity. Distances are marked in gray and pink, and the selected samples are marked in yellow.

According to **Figure 5**, first selecting the samples of greater dissimilarity, the teacher punctuates the most different ones and then some of the more similar ones.

As this teacher follows the ranking of samples suggested by the system, he himself can identify how far he can correct to obtain a minimum set of representation of the diversity of the solutions developed for composition of rubrics and, in the future, for to train automatic assessment exercises of programming exercises with a set of examples of teachers' marks. In this case, we consider 50% for training and 50% for testing of the prediction model.

Figure 6 presents our first prediction results performed at a distance learning C programming. In this graph, we present performance results of all the programming solutions developed by a student (*al_00009*) throughout a programming course. In the presentation of these results, for each submitted programming solution, we compared the grade given by a teacher with the grades predicted by our system from a history of activities previously solved by that same student and from solutions of other students of class in that same activity based on nearest neighbor methods. This process of performance analysis is performed for all students of the distance learning course through our system.

According to the graph of **Figure 6**, it is observed that the prediction of a student's performance in an activity based on a history of exercises solved by that student and in the solutions of that exercise developed by other students still present themselves divergent from the assigned marks by a teacher, although in higher performances these approaches approximate the evaluation of a teacher.

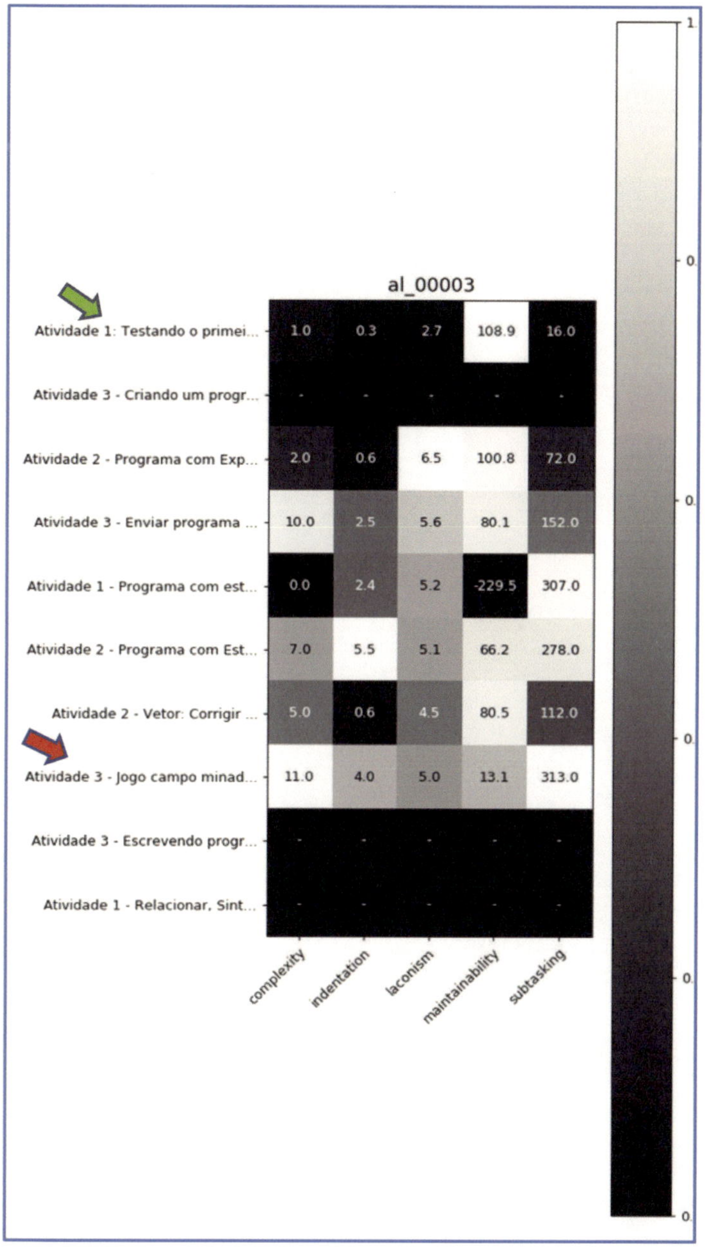

Figure 3.
Evolution of metrics for each activity.

In addition, the predictive results of these approaches approximate as the history of solved exercises used increases. Thus, we present good expectations to advance in the studies of these methods to predict the performance of programming students.

In conclusion, with some examples of the results generated by the system of this chapter, we shown the potential of this tool for programming teachers to accompany the process of learning their students from the beginning to the end of a course from a broad or reduced set of metrics and with less teachers' evaluation effort.

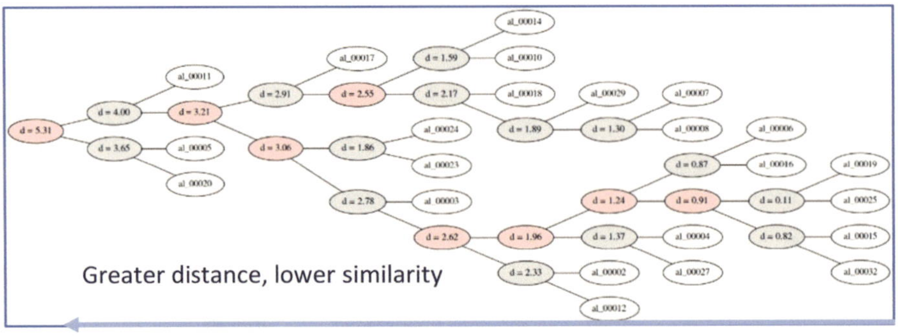

Figure 4.
Dendrogram of solutions of a programming activity represented on normalized software metrics (without grades).

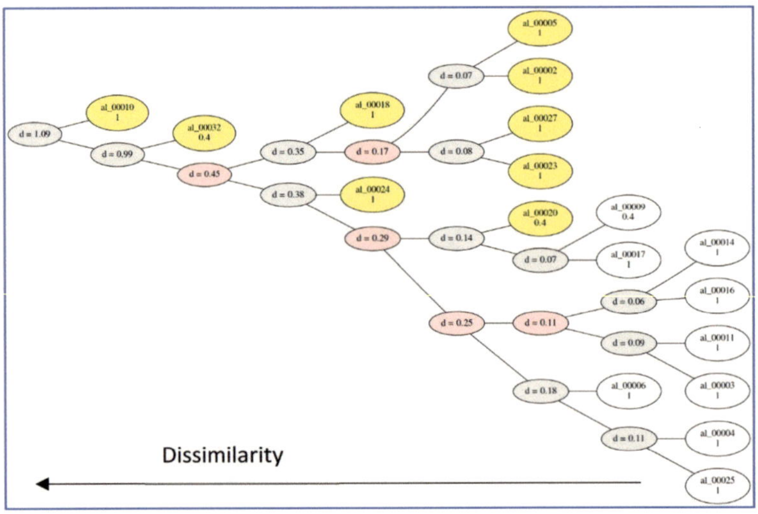

Figure 5.
Dendrogram of solutions of a programming activity selected from a correction ranking (with grades).

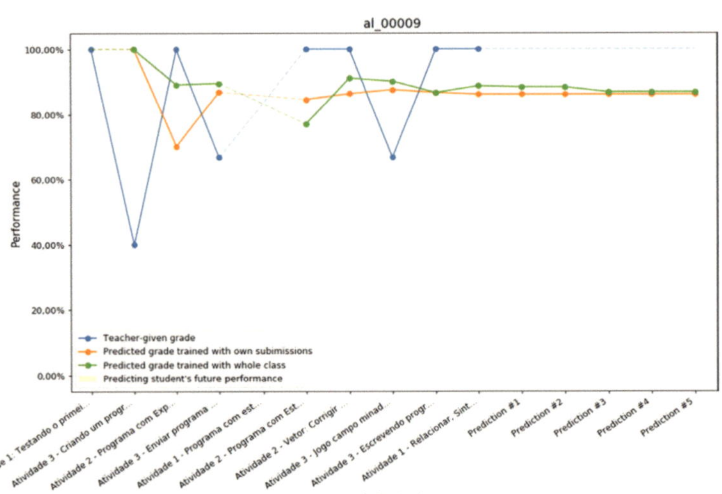

Figure 6.
Timeline with prediction of performance in programming.

5. Conclusion

The system proposed in this chapter was presented as a relevant tool to assist teachers in their evaluation decisions, enabling them to assist the learning process of their students in each programming exercise.

For this, our system can recognize where the learning difficulties begin, monitor how students evolve along a course, generate rubric representation and, soon, predict future performances of programming students.

These possibilities of learning analysis contribute a lot to reducing teachers' efforts in the onerous task of evaluating programming exercises so that they can better track the learning process of students and reorient their formative actions.

Some future works from this research are using samples indicated for manual correction as training references of a semi-automatic programming evaluation system and improving our strategy to predict performances in activities from the timeline of solved programming exercises or from students' solutions that solved exercises similar to the one we intend to predict a grade.

Through this work we offer, therefore, a multidimensional and the clinical analysis tool to help teachers in their formative assessment actions and students to be better assisted in their difficulties and skills in the practice of programming.

Author details

Márcia Gonçalves de Oliveira*, Ádler Oliveira Silva Neves
and Mônica Ferreira Silva Lopes
Federal Institute of Espírito Santo, Vitória, Espírito Santo, Brazil

*Address all correspondence to: marcia.oliveira@ifes.edu.br

References

[1] De Oliveira MG, Marques Ciarelli P, Oliveira E. Recommendation of programming activities by multi-label classification for a formative assessment of students. Expert Systems With Applications. 2013;**40**(16):6641-6651

[2] Ferreira Novais D, Varanda Pereira MJ, Rangel Henriques P. Profile detection through source code static analysis. Drops-Idn/6014. 2016;**51**(9):1-9

[3] Neves A, Reblin L, França H, Lopes M, Oliveira M, Oliveira E. Mapeamento Automático de Perfis de Estudantes em Métricas de Software para Análise de Aprendizagem de Programação. In Brazilian Symposium on Computers in Education (Simpósio Brasileiro de Informática na Educação-SBIE). 2017;**28**(1):1337

[4] Curtis B, Sheppard SB, Milliman P, Borst MA, Love T. Measuring the psychological complexity of software maintenance tasks with the Halstead and McCabe metrics. IEEE Transactions on Software Engineering. 1979;**5**(2):96-104

[5] Berry RE, Meekings BAE. A style analysis of C programs. Communications of the ACM. 1985;**28**:80-88

[6] Khirulnuzam AR, Ahmad S, Nordin J. The Design of an Automated C Programming Assessment Using Pseudo-code Comparison Technique. National Conference on Software Engineering and Computer Systems. 2007;1-10

[7] Xu S, Chee YS. Transformation-based diagnosis of student programs for programming tutoring systems. IEEE Transactions on Software Engineering. 2003;**29**:360-384

[8] Naude KA, Greyling JH, Vogts D. Marking student programs using graph similarity. Computers in Education. 2010;**54**(2):545-561

[9] Rees MJ. Automatic assessment aids for Pascal programs. SIGPLAN Notices. 1982;**17**(10):33-42

[10] Hung S, Kwok L, Chung A. New metrics for automated programming assessment. In: Proceedings of the IFIP WG34/SEARCC (SRIG on Education and Training) Working Conference on Software Engineering Education. Amsterdam, The Netherlands: North-Holland Publishing Co.; 1993. pp. 233-243

[11] de Oliveira MG, Reblin LL, de Souza MB, Oliveira E. Automatic recognition of rubric representations in programming exercises clusters. Brazilian Journal of Computers in Education. 2018;**26**(02):60

[12] Kumar V, Boulanger D, Seanosky J, Panneerselvam K, Somasundaram TS, et al. Competence analytics. Journal of Computers in Education. 2014;**1**(4):251-270

[13] Halstead MH. Elements of Software Science (Operating and Programming Systems Series). New York, NY, USA: Elsevier Science Inc.; 1977

[14] Blikstein P, Worsley M, Piech C, Sahami M, Cooper S, Koller D. Programming pluralism: Using learning analytics to detect patterns in the learning of computer programming. The Journal of the Learning Sciences. 2014;**23**(4):561-599

[15] Oliveira MG, Monroy NAJ, Zandonade E, Oliveira E. Análise de componentes latentes da aprendizagem

de programaçao para mapeamento e classificaçao de perfis. In Brazilian Symposium on Computers in Education (Simpósio Brasileiro de Informática na Educação-SBIE). 2014;**25**(1):134-143

[16] Oliveira M, França H, Neves A, Lopes M, Silva AC. Instrumentos de Visualização da Informação para Avaliação Diagnóstica em Curso de Programação a Distância. In: Anais do Workshop de Informática na Escola. October 2017;**23**(1):452

[17] Spalenza M, Oliveira E, Oliveira M, Nogueira M. Uso de Mapa de Características na Avaliação de Textos Curtos nos Ambientes Virtuais de Aprendizagem. In: Brazilian Symposium on Computers in Education (Simpósio Brasileiro de Informática na Educação-SBIE). 2016. p. 1165. Available from: http://www.br-ie.org/pub/index.php/sbie/article/view/6802

[18] Tang H, Xing W, Pei B. Time really matters: Understanding the temporal dimension of online learning using educational data mining. Journal of Educational Computing Research:0735633118784705. Available from: https://journals.sagepub.com/doi/pdf/10.1177/0735633118784705?casa_token=gYB8xtamE-AAAAAA:byyb5nlAyEnPrkI8u7gAtJNjn5Il4hysSOTAmSGBB1DLTCkjPJ3kqYm8Qy7iFTo3AHSfa59mDuAK5Q

[19] Pedregosa F, Varoquaux G, Gramfort A, Michel V, Thirion B, Grisel O, et al. Scikit-learn: Machine learning in python. Journal of Machine Learning Research. 2011;**12**:2825-2830. Available from: http://dl.acm.org/citation.cfm?id=2078195%5Cnhttp://arxiv.org/abs/1201.0490

Chapter 5

Multiset-Based Knowledge Representation for the Assessment and Optimization of Large-Scale Sociotechnical Systems

Igor Sheremet

Abstract

This chapter is dedicated to a new knowledge representation model, providing convergence of classical operations research and modern knowledge engineering. Kernel of the introduced model is the recursively generated multisets, selected according to the predefined restrictions and optimization criteria. Sets of multisets are described by the so-called multiset grammars (MGs), being projection of a conceptual background of well-known string-generating grammars on the multisets universum. Syntax and semantics of MGs and their practice-oriented development—unitary multiset grammars and metagrammars—are considered.

Keywords: systems analysis, operations research, knowledge engineering, digital economy, multisets, recursive multisets, multiset grammars, unitary multiset grammars and multimetagrammars, sociotechnical systems assessment and optimization

1. Introduction

Large-scale sociotechnical systems (STS) usually have hierarchical structure, including personnel and various technical devices, which, in turn, consume various material, financial, information resources, as well as energy. As a result, they produce new resources (objects), which are delivered to other similar systems. Main features of such STS are large dimensionality and high volatility of their structures, equipment, consumed/produced objects, and at all, operation logics and dynamics [1–5].

Knowledge and data representation models, used in STS, provide comparatively easy and comfortable management of very large knowledge and data bases with dynamic structures and content [6–10]. These model bases are objects other than matrices, vectors, and graphs, traditionally used in operations research and systems analysis [11–14], and they are much more convenient for practical problem consideration. But, on the other hand, aforementioned models in general case do not incorporate strict theoretical background and fundamental algorithmics, compared with, for example, mathematical programming, which provides strictly optimal solutions for decision-makers. So, practically all decision-support software in the considered STS is based on various heuristics, which correctness and adequacy are not proved usually in the mathematical sense. As a consequence, quality of the adopted decisions, based on such heuristics, in many cases may be far of optimal.

This chapter is dedicated to a primary survey of the developed knowledge representation model, providing convergence of classical operations research and modern knowledge engineering. This convergence creates new opportunities for complicated problem formalization and solution by integrating best features of mathematical programming (strict optimal solution search in solution space, defined by goal functions and boundary conditions) and constraint programming [15–17] (natural and easily updated top-down representation of logic of the decision-making in various situations). Kernel of the considered model is multisets (MS)—relatively long ago known and in the last 20 years intensively applied object of classical mathematics [18–29]. This background is generalized to the recursively generated, or, for short, recursive multisets (RMS) by introduction of so-called multiset grammars, or, again for short, multigrammars (MGs), which were described by the author in [30, 31]. Last, in turn, are peculiar "projection" of the conceptual basis of classical formal grammars by Chomsky [32, 33], operating strings of symbols, to the multisets universum in such a way, that MGs provide generation of one multiset from another and selection (filtration) of those, which satisfy necessary integral conditions: boundary restrictions and/or optimality criteria.

MGs may be considered as prolog-like constraint programming language for solution of problems in operations research and systems analysis areas. Taking into account relative novelty of the multigrammatical approach and absence of any substantial associations with mathematical constructions presented lower, we introduce main content of the chapter by short informal description of the main elements of this approach in Section 2. Basic formal definitions are presented in Section 3. Section 4 is dedicated to multiset grammars, while Section 5—to detailed consideration of the so-called unitary multigrammars (UMGs) and unitary multimetagrammars (UMMGs), which are main tool of the aforementioned problem formalization and solution.

2. Informal description

Let us consider a company, which consists of director, three departments, and one separate laboratory. This fact may be simply represented as follows:

$$company \rightarrow 1 \cdot director, 3 \cdot department, 1 \cdot laboratory. \tag{1}$$

In this notation, a whole structure of the company, detailed to employee positions, may be described in such a way:

$$\begin{aligned} department &\rightarrow 1 \cdot head - department, 3 \cdot laboratory, \\ laboratory &\rightarrow 1 \cdot head - laboratory, 2 \cdot analyst, 3 \cdot assistant. \end{aligned} \tag{2}$$

This set of constructions is of the form:

$$a \rightarrow n_1 \cdot a_1, \ldots, n_m \cdot a_m \tag{3}$$

describes following set, created by multiplying and summarizing quantities of identical positions:

$$\{1 \cdot director, 3 \cdot head - department, 10 \cdot head - laboratory, 20 \cdot analyst, 30 \cdot assistant\}, \tag{4}$$

where $n_i \cdot a_i$ means there are n_i positions of type a_i in this company.

Let us join to the company structure knowledge about employees' month salary, represented in the same unified manner:

$$\begin{aligned} &director \to 10000 \cdot eur, \\ &head\text{-}department \to 5000 \cdot eur, \\ &head\text{-}laboratory \to 3000 \cdot eur, \\ &analyst \to 1500 \cdot eur, \\ &assistant \to 500 \cdot eur. \end{aligned} \tag{5}$$

After applying to the joined set of constructions just the same multiplying-summarizing procedure, we may obtain resulting set containing the only element $\{100{,}000 \cdot eur\}$, which defines company's total financial resource, necessary for employees' provision a month.

Presented knowledge representation concerns systems analysis, that is, obtaining integral parameters of the system given its structure and local parameters.

Consider more sophisticated task-relating systems design and concerning development of company structure given its integral parameters. Goal is to determine rational quantity of departments and laboratories in the department, as well as quantities of analysts and assistants in one laboratory. Total salary is no more than 120,000 eur, quantity of analysts in one laboratory may be from 1 to 3, while corresponding quantity of assistants may be from 2 to 6. Total quantity of employees must be maximal. There may be three different variants of company structure: (1) three departments and one laboratory; (2) two departments and three laboratories; and (3) four departments. Corresponding set of constructions is as follows:

$$company \to 1 \cdot director, 3 \cdot department, 1 \cdot laboratory, \tag{6}$$

$$company \to 1 \cdot director, 2 \cdot department, 1 \cdot laboratory, \tag{7}$$

$$company \to 1 \cdot director, 4 \cdot department, \tag{8}$$

$$department \to 1 \cdot head\text{-}department, m \cdot laboratory, \tag{9}$$

$$laboratory \to 1 \cdot head\text{-}laboratory, n \cdot analyst, l \cdot assistant. \tag{10}$$

Constructions, defining employees' salary, and other aforementioned restrictions are as follows (for definiteness, let us take that quantity of laboratories in one department does not exceed five):

$$director \to 1 \cdot employee, 10000 \cdot eur, \tag{11}$$

$$head\text{-}department \to 1 \cdot employee, \ 5000 \cdot eur, \tag{12}$$

$$head\text{-}laboratory \to 1 \cdot employee, \ 3000 \cdot eur, \tag{13}$$

$$analyst \to 1 \cdot employee, \ 1500 \cdot eur, \tag{14}$$

$$assistant \to 1 \cdot employee, \ 500 \cdot eur, \tag{15}$$

$$employee = \max, \tag{16}$$

$$eur \leq 120000, \tag{17}$$

$$1 \leq m \leq 5, \tag{18}$$

$$1 \leq n \leq 3, \tag{19}$$

$$1 \leq l \leq 6. \tag{20}$$

As seen, along with already introduced "detailing" constructions, there are additional constructions, defining sets of values of variables, having places in the first ones, as well as conditions, determining optimization criterion (there may be several such criteria), and bounds of quantities of some objects in the resulting sets. Evidently, due to presence of alternatives in the description of company structure (there are three such alternatives) and variables in some of "detailing" constructions, there may be more than one resulting set like Eq. (4). These sets are of the form $\{x \cdot employee, y \cdot eur\}$, where x is the quantity of employees, while y—total salary, corresponding to this variant. Conditions (16)–(20) provide selection of those sets, which satisfy them in the described sense. In general, Eqs. (16)–(20) may be interpreted as a query, determining subset of all possible variants, described by Eqs. (6)–(15).

To "mark" "detailing" constructions, used while resulting set creation, one can add to their "bodies" elements like $1 \cdot variant\text{-i}$, for example,

$$company \to 1 \cdot variant\text{-}1, 1 \cdot director, 3 \cdot department, 1 \cdot laboratory, \tag{21}$$

$$company \to 1 \cdot variant\text{-}2, 1 \cdot director, 2 \cdot department, 3 \cdot laboratory, \tag{22}$$

$$company \to 1 \cdot variant\text{-}3, 1 \cdot director, 4 \cdot department. \tag{23}$$

If so, then resulting sets will be of the form:

$$\{1 \cdot variant\text{-i}, \mathrm{x} \cdot employee, y \cdot eur\}. \tag{24}$$

To implant to these sets values of variables, it is sufficient to represent them in resulting sets in "usual" form $j \cdot v$, where v is variable and j is its value, so considered example will lead us to sets like:

$$\{1 \cdot variant\text{-i}, \mathrm{x} \cdot employee, y \cdot eur, i \cdot m, j \cdot n, k \cdot l\}. \tag{25}$$

As seen, shortly introduced by this example knowledge and query representation language, being easy to understand and to use, allows formalization of multicriterial optimization problems, for years associated with mathematical programming. On the other hand, "detailing" constructions have form of productions (rules), far and wide used in knowledge engineering and being common background of prolog-like declarative (nonprocedural) knowledge representation [34–36]. As will be shown lower, such constructions may be used not only for structuring, but in many other cases, enabling description of various systems behavior and interaction, as well as their mutual impacts. For such reasons, this informally described technique is taken as a basis for the description of the developed mathematical toolkit considered thoroughly in the following sections.

3. Basic operations on multisets

Classical set theory is based on the concept of set as unordered assembly of elements, different from one another. Theory of multisets assumes presence of equal ("indistinguishable") elements:

$$v = \left\{ \underbrace{a_1, \ldots, a_1}_{n_1\ times}, \ldots, \underbrace{a_i, \ldots, a_i}_{n_i\ times}, \ldots, \underbrace{a_m, \ldots, a_m}_{n_m\ times} \right\} \tag{26}$$

Expression (26) is recorded as:

$$v = \{n_1 \cdot a_1, \dots, n_m \cdot a_m\}, \tag{27}$$

where v is called multiset, $a_1, \dots, a_m$—objects, $n_1, \dots, n_m$—multiplicities of these objects, and $n_1 \cdot a_1, \dots, n_m \cdot a_m$—multiobjects. Following Eq. (27), one may consider v as set of multiobjects; also, from substantial point of view, set $\{a_1, \dots, a_m\}$ and multiset $\{1 \cdot a_1, \dots, 1 \cdot a_m\}$ are equivalent. Empty multiset, as well as empty set, is designated as $\{\varnothing\}$. Multiplicity of object may be zero, what is equivalent to absence of this object in the multiset:

$$\{n_1 \cdot a_1, \dots, n_m \cdot a_m, 0 \cdot a_{m+1}\} = \{n_1 \cdot a_1, \dots, n_m \cdot a_m\}. \tag{28}$$

Fact that object a or multiobject $n \cdot a$ belongs to multiset v ("enters v") is designated by one and the same symbol $\in$: $a \in v, n \cdot a \in v$. Set $\beta(v) = \{a | n \cdot a \in v\}$ is called basis of multiset v.

There are five main operations on multisets, used lower: join, intersection, addition, subtraction, and multiplication by constant [26, 27].

Consider two multisets:

$$\begin{aligned} v &= \{n_1 \cdot a_1, \dots, n_m \cdot a_m\}, \\ v' &= \{n'_1 \cdot a'_1, \dots, n'_{m'} \cdot a'_{m'}\}. \end{aligned} \tag{29}$$

Result of their join (recorded as $\cup$) is multiset.

$$\begin{aligned} v \bigcup v' = & \left(\bigcup_{\substack{a \in \{a_1, \dots, a_m\} \cap \{a'_1, \dots, a'_{m'}\} \\ n \cdot a \in v \\ n' \cdot a \in v}} \{\max(n, n') \cdot a\} \right) \cup \\ & \cup \left(\bigcup_{\substack{a \in \{a_1, \dots, a'_{m'}\} - \{a'_1, \dots, a'_{m'}\} \\ n \cdot a \in v}} \{n \cdot a\} \right) \cup \\ & \cup \left(\bigcup_{\substack{a' \in \{a'_1, \dots, a'_m\} - \{a_1, \dots, a_m\} \\ n' \cdot a' \in v}} \{n' \cdot a'\} \right), \end{aligned} \tag{30}$$

where $\cup$, $\cap$ and$-$ designate operations of set-theoretical join, intersection, and subtraction of two sets correspondingly, while $\bigcup$ designates operation of set-theoretical join of sets determined by underwritten conditions.

Result of v, v' multisets intersection (recorded as $\bigcap$) is multiset.

$$v \bigcap v' = \left(\bigcup_{\substack{a \in \{a_1, \dots, a_m\} \cap \{a'_1, \dots, a'_{m'}\} \\ n \cdot a \in v \\ n' \cdot a \in v}} \{\min(n, n') \cdot a\} \right). \tag{31}$$

Result of v, v' multisets addition (recorded as bold +) is multiset.

$$v+v' = \left(\bigcup_{\substack{a \in \{a_1, ..., a_m\} \cap \{a'_1, ..., a'_{m'}\} \\ n \cdot a \in v \\ n' \cdot a \in v}} \{(n+n') \cdot a\} \right) \cup \left(\bigcup_{\substack{a \in \{a_1, ..., a_m\} - \{a'_1, ..., a'_{m'}\} \\ n \cdot a \in v}} \{n \cdot a\} \right) \cup \left(\bigcup_{\substack{a' \in \{a'_1, ..., a'_{m'}\} - \{a_1, ..., a_m\} \\ n' \cdot a \in v'}} \{n' \cdot a\} \right). \quad (32)$$

Result of v' multiset subtraction from v multiset (recorded as bold −) is multiset.

$$v - v' = \left(\bigcup_{\substack{a \in \{a_1, ..., a_m\} \cap \{a'_1, ..., a'_{m'}\} \\ n \cdot a \in v \\ n' \cdot a \in v' \\ n > n'}} \{(n-n') \cdot a\} \right) \cup \left(\bigcup_{\substack{a \in \{a_1, ..., a_m\} - \{a'_1, ..., a'_{m'}\} \\ n \cdot a \in v}} \{n \cdot a\} \right). \quad (33)$$

At last, result of v multiset multiplication by integer number n (recorded as $v*n$) is multiset.

$$v*n = \{(n \times n_1) \cdot a_1, ..., (n \times n_m) \cdot a_m\} \quad (34)$$

(here integers' usual multiplication is recorded as $\times$)

There are also two basic relations on multisets: inclusion ($\subseteq$) and strict inclusion ($\subset$).

Multiset v is included to multiset v', that is, $v \subseteq v'$, if

$$(\forall n \cdot a \in v)[((\exists n' \cdot a \in v')\, n \leq n')], \quad (35)$$

and multiset v is strictly included to multiset v', that is, $v \subset v'$, if $v \subseteq v'$ & $v \neq v'$.

Example 1. Let $v_1 = \{3 \bullet analyst, 2 \bullet assistant\}$, $v_2 = \{4 \bullet assistant, 1 \bullet director\}$, then

$$v_1 \cup v_2 = \{3 \cdot analyst, 4 \cdot assistant, 1 \cdot director\},$$
$$v_1 \cap v_2 = \{2 \cdot assistant\},$$
$$v_1 + v_2 = \{3 \cdot analyst, 6 \cdot assistant, 1 \cdot director\},$$
$$v_2 - v_1 = \{2 \cdot assistant\},$$
$$v_1 * 2 = \{6 \cdot analyst, 4 \cdot assistant\},$$
$$\{1 \cdot analyst, 2 \cdot assistant\} \subset v_1,$$
$$\{4 \cdot assistant, 1 \cdot director\} \subseteq v_2. \blacksquare$$

All defined operations are known from widespread sources (e.g., aforementioned [26, 27]). At the same time, filtering operations, defined lower, operate sets of multisets (SMS), creating subsets of these sets by selection of multisets, which satisfy some conditions, being operands of these operations.

There are two types of conditions: boundary and optimizing.

Boundary condition may be elementary or concatenated (for short, "chain"). Elementary boundary condition (EBC) may have one of the following forms:

$$n \rho a, \quad (36)$$

$$a \rho n, \quad (37)$$

$$a \rho a', \quad (38)$$

where a and a' are the objects, n is the integer number, and $\rho \in \{<, =, \leq\}$. Chain boundary condition (CBC) is constructed from elementary by writing them sequentially:

$$e_1 \rho_1 e_2 \rho_2 \ldots e_i \rho_i e_{i+1} \ldots e_m \rho_m e_{m+1}, \quad (39)$$

where $e_1, \ldots, e_{m+1}$ are the objects or nonnegative integers, while $\rho_1, \ldots, \rho_m$ are the symbols of relations $(<, =, \leq)$.

EBC semantics is following. Let V be set of multisets, and $v \in V$. Multiset v satisfies EBC $\overline{n} \rho a$, if $n \cdot a \in V$, and $\overline{n} \rho n$ is true. Similarly, v satisfies EBC $a \rho \overline{n}$, if $\overline{n} \rho n$ is also true. At last, v satisfies EBC $a \rho a'$, if $n \cdot a \in v$, $n' \cdot a' \in v$, and $n \rho n'$ is true. There is one addition to all listed definitions, concerning particular case, when $n \cdot a \notin v \ (n' \cdot a \notin v)$, which is equivalent to $n = 0 \ (n' = 0)$.

CBC semantics is defined as follows. CBC (39) is replaced by CBC sequence

$$e_1 \rho_1 e_2, e_2 \rho_2 e_3, \ldots, e_i \rho_i e_{i+1}, \ldots, e_m \rho_m e_{m+1}, \quad (40)$$

and $v \in V$ is considered satisfying CBC (39), if it satisfies all EBC having place in Eq. (40).

Result of application of boundary condition b to SMS V is recorded as $V \downarrow b$.

Example 2. Let $V = \{v_1, v_2\}$, where $v_1 = \{5 \cdot analyst, 3 \cdot assistant, 1 \cdot director\}$, $v_2 = \{2 \cdot assistant, 4 \cdot director, 3 \cdot employee\}$, and boundary conditions are $2 \leq analyst \leq 4$, $assistant < employee$, $1 \leq director \leq assistant \leq 3$, and $analyst = assistant < 5$. **Table 1** contains result of application of listed boundary conditions to V.$\blacksquare$

Optimizing condition has form $a = opt$, where a is the object, and $opt \in \{\min, \max\}$. Semantics of this construction is following. Multiset $v \in V$ satisfies condition $a = \min$, if for every $v' \in V$, such that $v \neq v'$, multiplicity n in multiobject $n \cdot a \in v$ is not greater, than multiplicity n' in multiobject $n' \cdot a \in v'$, that is, $n \leq n'$. Similarly, $v \in V$ satisfies condition $a = \max$, if for every $v' \in V$, such that $v \neq v'$, multiplicity n in multiobject $n \cdot a \in v$ is not less, than multiplicity n' in

condition	$V \downarrow condition$
$2 \le analyst \le 4$	$\{v_2\}$
$assistant < employee$	$\{v_2\}$
$1 \le director \le assistant \le 3$	$\{v_1\}$
$analyst = assistant < 5$	$\{\varnothing\}$

Table 1.
Results of application of boundary conditions.

multiobject $n' \cdot a \in v'$, that is, $n \ge n'$. If $a \notin v$ $(a' \notin v)$, we consider $n \cdot a \in v$ $(n' \cdot a \in v)$, where $n = 0$ $(n' = 0)$.

Filter is join of boundary $F_{\le}$ and optimizing F_{opt} subfilters:

$$F = F_{\le} \cup F_{opt}, \tag{41}$$

where $F_{\le}$ is set of boundary conditions, and F_{opt} is set of optimizing conditions. Result of filtration of set of multisets V by filter F is denoted as $V \downarrow F$ and is defined by expression

$$V \downarrow F = (V \downarrow F_{\le}) \downarrow F_{opt} \tag{42}$$

where

$$F_{\le} = \{c_1, \dots, c_k\}, \tag{43}$$

$$F_{opt} = \{opt_1, \dots, \mathrm{opt}_l\}, \tag{44}$$

$$V \downarrow F_{\le} = \bigcap_{i=1}^{k} (V \downarrow c_i) = V', \tag{45}$$

$$V' \downarrow F_{opt} = \bigcap_{j=1}^{l} \left(V' \downarrow opt_j\right), \tag{46}$$

and $c_1, \dots, c_k$ are EBC. As seen, set V is filtered by boundary conditions, so there are selected multisets, satisfying all of these conditions, and intermediate result V' is then filtered by optimizing conditions, so, that multisets, satisfying all of them, are included to the final result.

Example 3. Consider set $V = \{v_1, v_2, v_3, v_4\}$, where

$$\begin{aligned} v_1 &= \{3 \cdot analyst, 2 \cdot assistant, 2 \cdot employee\}, \\ v_2 &= \{6 \cdot assistant, 2 \cdot director\}, \\ v_3 &= \{1 \cdot analyst, 3 \cdot assistant, 5 \cdot director, 2 \cdot employee\}, \\ v_4 &= \{1 \cdot analyst, 2 \cdot assistant, 2 \cdot employee\}. \end{aligned}$$

Let $F = \{1 \le analyst \le 3, 2 \le director \le employee, analyst = \min, assistant = \max\}$. Then, according to Eqs. (41)–(46),

$$V \downarrow F = (V \downarrow F_{\le}) \downarrow F_{opt},$$

where

$$\begin{aligned} F_{\le} &= \{1 \le analyst \le 3, 2 \le director \le employee\}, \\ F_{opt} &= \{assistant = \min, employee = \max\}. \end{aligned}$$

Filtration is performed as follows:

$$V \downarrow \{1 \le analyst \le 3\} = \{v_1, v_3, v_4\},$$
$$V \downarrow \{2 \le director \le 4\} = \{v_1, v_2, v_4\},$$
$$V \downarrow F_{\le} = \{v_1, v_4\},$$
$$\{v_1, v_4\} \downarrow \{assistant = \min\} = \{v_1\},$$
$$\{v_1, v_4\} \downarrow \{employee = \max\} = \{v_1, v_4\},$$
$$V \downarrow F = \{v_1\} \cap \{v_1, v_4\} = \{v_1\}. \blacksquare$$

Due to commutativity of set-theoretic join and intersection operations, filtration inside subfilters may be executed in the arbitrary order.

4. Multiset grammars

As mentioned higher, multiset grammars are tool, providing generation of one multisets from another, or, what is the same, generation sets of multisets.

By analogy with classical grammars, operating strings of symbols [32, 33], we shall define multigrammar as a couple.

$$S = \langle v_0, R \rangle, \tag{47}$$

where v_0 is a multiset called kernel, while R, called scheme, is finite set of the so-called rules, which are used for generation of new multisets from already generated. Rule has the form:

$$v \to v', \tag{48}$$

where v (left part of the rule) and v' (right part of the rule) are multisets, and $v \neq \{\emptyset\}$. Semantics of rule is as follows. Let $\overline{v}$ be multiset; with that we shall speak, that rule (48) is applicable to $\overline{v}$, if $v \subseteq \overline{v}$, and result of its application is a multiset.

$$\overline{v}' = \overline{v} - v + v'. \tag{49}$$

Speaking informally, if $\overline{v}$ includes v, then the last is replaced by v'. Application of rule $r \in R$ to multiset $\overline{v}$ is denoted as $\overline{v} \overset{r}{\Rightarrow} \overline{v'}$, and any sequence $\overline{v} \overset{r}{\Rightarrow} \ldots \overset{r'}{\Rightarrow} \overline{v'}$ is called generation chain.

Set of multisets, defined by MGs $S = \langle v_0, R \rangle$, is denoted as V_S. Iterative representation of MG semantics, that is, SMS V_S generation by application of MG S, is the following:

$$V_{(0)} = \{v_0\}, \tag{50}$$

$$V_{(i+1)} = V_{(i)} \cup \left(\bigcup_{\overline{v} \in V_{(i)}} \bigcup_{r \in R} \pi(\overline{v}, r) \right), \tag{51}$$

$$V_S = V_{(\infty)}, \tag{52}$$

where

$$\pi(\overline{v}, v \to v') = \begin{cases} \{\overline{v} - v + v'\}, \textit{if } v \subseteq \overline{v}, \\ \{\emptyset\} \textit{ otherwise}. \end{cases} \tag{53}$$

As seen, function (53) implements application of rule $v \rightarrow v'$ to multiset $\overline{v}$ as described higher. As a result of i + 1-th step of generation, new SMS is formed by application of all rules $r \in R$ to all multisets $\overline{v} \in V_{(i)}$, and it is joined to SMS $V_{(i)}$. If multiset $\overline{v'}$ is generated from multiset $\overline{v}$ by some sequence of such steps, it is denoted as $\overline{v} \overset{*}{\Rightarrow} \overline{v'}$.

V_S is fixed point of the described process, that is, $V_S = V_{(i)}$, where $i \rightarrow \infty$. If for some finite i $V_{(i)} = V_{(i+1)}$, then $V_S = V_{(i)}$, and V_S is finite. In the introduced notation,

$$V_S = \left\{ v | v_0 \overset{*}{\Rightarrow} v \right\}. \tag{54}$$

V_S includes subset $\overline{V}_s \subseteq V_s$ of the so-called terminal multisets (TMS) $v \in \overline{V}_s$ such that $\pi(v, r) = \{\varnothing\}$ for all $r \in R$, that is, no one multiset may be generated from terminal multiset. Set $\overline{V}_S$ is called final; final set consists of terminal multisets only.

Example 4. Let $S = \langle v_0, R \rangle$, where $v_0 = \{3 \cdot eur, 4 \cdot usd\}$,
$R = \{r_1, r_2\}$, where
r_1 is $\{2 \cdot eur, 1 \cdot usd\} \rightarrow \{1 \cdot eur, 1 \cdot gbp\}$,
r_2 is $\{1 \cdot eur, 2 \cdot usd\} \rightarrow \{1 \cdot eur, 2 \cdot gbp\}$.
As seen,

$$v_0 = \{3 \cdot eur, 4 \cdot usd\} \overset{r_1}{\Rightarrow} \{2 \cdot eur, 3 \cdot usd, 1 \cdot gbp\} \overset{r_1}{\Rightarrow} \{1 \cdot eur, 2 \cdot usd, 2 \cdot gbp\} \overset{r_2}{\Rightarrow} \{1 \cdot usd, 4 \cdot gbp\},$$

$$\{2 \cdot eur, 3 \cdot usd, 1 \cdot gbp\} \overset{r_2}{\Rightarrow} \{1 \cdot a_1, 2 \cdot usd, 3 \cdot gbp\} \overset{r_2}{\Rightarrow} \{1 \cdot usd, 5 \cdot gbp\},$$

$$\{3 \cdot eur, 4 \cdot usd\} \overset{r_2}{\Rightarrow} \{2 \cdot eur, 3 \cdot usd, 2 \cdot gbp\} \overset{r_1}{\Rightarrow} \{1 \cdot eur, 2 \cdot usd, 3 \cdot gbp\} \overset{r_2}{\Rightarrow} \{1 \cdot usd, 5 \cdot gbp\},$$

$$\{2 \cdot eur, 3 \cdot usd, 2 \cdot gbp\} \overset{r_2}{\Rightarrow} \{1 \cdot eur, 2 \cdot usd, 4 \cdot gbp\} \overset{r_2}{\Rightarrow} \{1 \cdot usd, 6 \cdot gbp\}$$

(for short, identical parts of different generation chains are omitted). So

$$\overline{V}_s = \{\{1 \cdot eur, 4 \cdot gbp\}, \{1 \cdot usd, 5 \cdot gbp\}, \{1 \cdot usd, 6 \cdot gbp\}\} \ \blacksquare.$$

By analogy with classical string-generating grammars, multigrammars may be context-sensitive and context-free (CF). In the last one, left parts of all rules have form $\{1 \cdot a\}$, while in the first, there are no any limitations on both parts of rules, excluding, that left part must be nonempty multiset.

5. Unitary multiset grammars and metagrammars

Start point for unitary multigrammars (UMGs), developed on the considered basis, is simplified representation of CF rules: instead of

$$\{1 \cdot a\} \rightarrow \{n_1 \cdot a_1, ..., n_m \cdot a_m\} \tag{55}$$

they are written as:

$$a \rightarrow n_1 \cdot a_1, ..., n_m \cdot a_m. \tag{56}$$

Construction (56) is called unitary rule (UR), object a—its head, and unordered sequence (list) $n_1 \cdot a_1, ..., n_m \cdot a_m$—its body.

Let us consider UMG formal definition and illustrating example. Unitary multigrammar is couple $S = \langle a_0, R \rangle$, where a is the so-called title object, and R, as in multigrammars, is scheme—set of unitary rules (56).

Iterative representation of UMG semantics, i.e., generation of SMS V_S, where $S = \langle a_0, R \rangle$, is following:

$$V_{(0)} = \{1 \cdot a_0\}, \tag{57}$$

$$V_{(i+1)} = V_{(i)} \cup \bigcup_{\overline{v} \in V_{(i)}} \bigcup_{r \in R} \{\overline{\pi}(\overline{v}, r)\}, \tag{58}$$

$$V_S = V_{(\infty)}, \tag{59}$$

$$\overline{V}_S = \{\overline{v} | \overline{v} \in V_S \,\&\, \beta(\overline{v}) \subseteq \overline{A}_s\}, \tag{60}$$

where

$$\overline{\pi}(\overline{v}, \langle a \to n_1 \cdot a_1, ..., n_m \cdot a_m \rangle) = \begin{cases} \overline{v} - \{n \cdot a\} + n * \{n_1 \cdot a_1, ..., n_m \cdot a_m\}, \text{ if } n \cdot a \in \overline{v}, \\ \{\varnothing\} \text{ otherwise}. \end{cases} \tag{61}$$

Here, $\overline{A}_s$ is set of the so-called terminal objects, such that $a \in \overline{A}_s$, if and only if R does not include URs, which head is a (i.e., a has place only in the UR bodies). $\overline{A}_s$ is subset of set A_s of all objects, having places in scheme R of UMG S. Multiset, generated by UMG S, all objects of which are terminal, is also called terminal multiset (as seen, this notion of TMS does not contradict to the defined higher regarding MGs). In Eq. (61), UR $a \to n_1 \cdot a_1, \cdots, n_m \cdot a_m$ is written in the angle brackets for unambiguity.

As seen, Eq. (59) defines V_S—set of all multisets, generated by UMG S,—while Eq. (60) by condition $\beta(\overline{v}) \subseteq \overline{A}_s$ provides selection of $\overline{V}_S$—set of terminal multisets (STMS)—from V_S.

Example 5. Consider unitary multigrammar $S = \langle company, R \rangle$, where R includes following unitary rules:

$$\begin{aligned} &company \to 3 \cdot group, 2 \cdot analyst, \\ &company \to 3 \cdot analyst, \\ &group \to 1 \cdot analyst, \\ &group \to 2 \cdot analyst. \end{aligned}$$

According to Eqs. (57)–(61),

$$\begin{aligned} &V_S = \{\{1 \cdot company\}, \{3 \cdot group, 2 \cdot analyst\}, \{3 \cdot analyst\}, \{5 \cdot analyst\}, \{8 \cdot analyst\}\}, \\ &\overline{V}_S = \{\{3 \cdot analyst\}, \{5 \cdot analyst\}, \{8 \cdot analyst\}\}. \;\blacksquare \end{aligned}$$

Filtering unitary multigrammars (FUMGs) are UMG generalization, providing generation of terminal multisets and selection those of them, which satisfy conditions, assembled to filters, which were described higher in Section 3.

FUMGs are triple $S = \langle a_0, R, F \rangle$, where a_0, R, and F have the same sense, as above, and set of terminal multisets, generated by S, is defined as follows:

$$\overline{V}_S = \overline{V}_{\langle a_0, R \rangle} \downarrow F, \tag{62}$$

that is, set of terminal multisets, generated by S, is result of filtering STMS, generated by UMGs $\langle a_0, R \rangle$, by filter F.

Example 6. Let $S = \langle company, R, F \rangle$, where R is as in Example 5, while $F = \{analyst > 3, analyst = \min\}$. Then, according to Eqs. (57)–(62),

$$\overline{V}_S = (\{\{3 \cdot analyst\}, \{5 \cdot a_2\}analyst, \{8 \cdot analyst\}\} \downarrow \{analyst>3\}) \downarrow \{analyst = \min\}$$
$$= (\{\{5 \cdot analyst\}, \{8 \cdot analyst\}\}) \downarrow \{analyst = \min\} = \{\{5 \cdot analyst\}\}. \blacksquare$$

Filtering unitary multigrammars are, in turn, basis for unitary multiset metagrammars, or, for short, multimetagrammars, which are considered at all the rest part of the chapter and are main toolkit for the description and solution of the optimization problems, mentioned in the introduction.

Unitary multimetagrammar S is, as higher, triple $\langle a_0, R, F\rangle$, where a_0 is the title object, and R is the scheme, containing unitary rules and so-called unitary metarules (UMR), while F is the filter. Consider UMMG syntax and semantics.

Unitary metarule has the form:

$$a \rightarrow \mu_1 \cdot a_1, ..., \mu_m \cdot a_m, \tag{63}$$

where μ_i is the positive integer number, as in UMGs/FUMGs, or variable $\gamma \in \Gamma$, where Γ is the universum of variables. When μ_i is $\gamma_i \in \Gamma$, then it is called multiplicity-variable (MV). As seen, unitary rule is the simplest particular case of unitary metarule with all multiplicities $\mu_1, ..., \mu_m$ being constants. As in URs, object a in Eq. (55) is called head, while $\mu_1 \cdot a_1, ..., \mu_m \cdot a_m$—body of metarule.

Filter F is set of conditions, which may be of the following forms:

$$n \leq a \leq n', \tag{64}$$

$$a = opt, \tag{65}$$

$$n \leq \gamma \leq n', \tag{66}$$

where $opt \in \{\max, \min\}$. As seen, boundary condition (64) and optimizing condition (65) are the same, as in FUMG filters, while boundary condition (65), called variable declaration, defines set of values (domain) of variable γ and is denoted lower as $N(\gamma)$. If F includes subfilter $F_\Gamma = \{n_1 \leq \gamma_1 \leq n'_1, ..., n_l \leq \gamma_l \leq n'_l\}$, containing boundary conditions of form (66), then every combination of variable values $\overline{n}_1 \in N(\gamma_1), ..., \overline{n}_l \in N(\gamma_l)$ provides creation of one unitary multigrammar by substitution of $\overline{n}_1, ..., \overline{n}_l$ to all unitary metarules, having places in scheme R, instead of multiplicities-variables being in their bodies; unitary rules, already having place in R, are transferred to new scheme, denoted $R\circ\langle\overline{n}_1, ..., \overline{n}_l\rangle$, without any transformations. Every such UMGs generates set of terminal multisets, after what all these STMS are joined, and resulting set is filtered by filter $F = F - F_\Gamma$, containing all "FUMG-like" conditions (From the described, it is obvious nature of "multimetagrammar" notion—in mathematical logic, or "metamathematics," "metalanguage" is language, used for description of another language, so "multimetagrammar" is "unitary-like" multigrammar, used for description of other unitary multigrammars by means of unitary metarules, variables-multiplicities, and boundary conditions, defining their domains.). As may be seen from this informal description, UMMGs are simple unified tool for compact representation of sets of FUMGs (for practically valuable problems, containing very large numbers of elements—millions and greater).

Coming back to Section 2, one can see that Eqs. (6)–(20) are set of elements of unitary metamultigrammar: Eqs. (6)–(8) and Eqs. (11)–(15) are unitary rules, Eqs. (9)–(10) are unitary metarules, Eq. (16) is optimizing condition, Eq. (17) is boundary condition, while Eqs. (18)–(20) are variable declarations. As seen,

$$N(m) = \{1, 2, 3, 4, 5\}, \tag{67}$$

$$N(n) = \{1, 2, 3\}, \tag{68}$$

$$N(l) = \{1, 2, 3, 4, 5, 6\}, \tag{69}$$

so, this one UMMG, consisting of 15 lines, replaces $5 \times 3 \times 5 = 75$ filtering unitary multigrammars, each scheme consisting of 10 lines.

Let us now give strict definition of unitary multimetagrammar notion. UMMG $S = \langle a_0, R, F \rangle$ defines set of terminal multisets $\overline{V}_S$ in such a way:

$$\overline{V}_S = \left(\bigcup_{\overline{S} \in S^*} \overline{V}_{\overline{S}} \right) \downarrow \mathrm{F}, \tag{70}$$

$$S^* = \bigcup_{\gamma_1 \in n_1}^{n'_1} \dots \bigcup_{\gamma_l \in n_l}^{n'_l} \{\langle a_0, R \circ \langle \gamma_1, \dots, \gamma_l \rangle \rangle\}, \tag{71}$$

$$R \circ \langle \overline{n}_1, \dots, \overline{n}_l \rangle = \{ r \circ \langle \overline{n}_1, \dots, \overline{n}_l \rangle | r \in R \}, \tag{72}$$

$$\mathrm{F} = F - F_\Gamma, \tag{73}$$

$$F_\Gamma = \bigcup_{i=1}^{l} \{ n_i \leq \gamma_i \leq n'_i \}, \tag{74}$$

and, at last, if r is $a \leftarrow \mu_1 \cdot a_1, \dots, \mu_m \cdot a_m$, then $r \circ \langle \overline{n}_1, \dots, \overline{n}_l \rangle$ is unitary rule.

$$a \leftarrow (\mu_1 \circ \langle \overline{n}_1, \dots, \overline{n}_l \rangle) \cdot a_1, \dots, (\mu_m \circ \langle \overline{n}_1, \dots, \overline{n}_l \rangle) \cdot a_m, \tag{75}$$

where

$$\mu_i \circ \langle \overline{n}_1, \dots, \overline{n}_l \rangle = \begin{cases} \mu_i, \text{ if } \mu_i \in \boldsymbol{N}, \\ \overline{n}_j, \text{ if } \mu_i \text{ is } \gamma_j \in \Gamma. \end{cases} \tag{76}$$

As seen, according to Eqs. (75) and (76), all multiplicities-variables of unitary metarule $a \leftarrow \mu_1 \cdot a_1, \dots, \mu_m \cdot a_m$ are replaced by their corresponding values from the tuple $\langle \overline{n}_1, \dots, \overline{n}_l \rangle$, while all multiplicities-constants (elements of positive integer numbers set $\boldsymbol{N}$) remain unchanged. Evidently, if all $\mu_1, \dots, \mu_m$ are constants, that is, if unitary metarule is UR, it remains unchanged.

Let us note, that multiplicities-variables area of actuality is whole UMMG scheme, that is, if there are $n > 1$ occurrences of one and the same variable γ in different unitary metarules (and, of course, in one and the same unitary metarule), they all are substituted by one and the same value from the applied sequence $\langle \overline{n}_1, \dots, \overline{n}_l \rangle$.

Example 7. Let us consider UMMG $S = <$*company, R, F*$>$, where scheme R contains following three unitary metarules:

$$\begin{aligned} &company \to 2 \cdot group, \gamma_1 \cdot analyst, \\ &group \to 3 \cdot analyst, \gamma_2 \cdot assistant, \\ &group \to \gamma_1 \cdot analyst, \gamma_2 \cdot assistant, \end{aligned}$$

and filter F includes following conditions, the first being boundary, the second—optimizing, while the last two—variable declarations:

$$\begin{aligned} &2 \leq analyst \leq 6, \\ &assistant = \min, \\ &0 \leq \gamma_1 \leq 1, \\ &2 \leq \gamma_2 \leq 3. \end{aligned}$$

According to Eqs. (70)–(76), this UMMG defines four UMGs:

$$S_{0,2} = <company, Ro<0,2>>,$$
$$S_{0,3} = <company, Ro<0,3>>,$$
$$S_{1,2} = <company, Ro<1,2>>,$$
$$S_{1,3} = <company, Ro<1,3>>,$$

where

$$Ro<0,2> = \{<company \to 2 \cdot group>, <group \to 3 \cdot analyst, 2 \cdot assistant>, <group_1 \to 2 \cdot assistant>\},$$
$$Ro<0,3> = \{<company \to 2 \cdot group>, <group \to 3 \cdot analyst, 3 \cdot assistant>, <group \to 3 \cdot assistant>\},$$
$$Ro<1,2> = \{<company \to 2 \cdot group, 1 \cdot analyst>, <group \to 3 \cdot analyst, 2 \cdot assistant>, <group \to 1 \cdot analyst, 2 \cdot assistant>\},$$
$$Ro<1,3> = \{<company \to 2 \cdot group, 1 \cdot analyst>, <group \to 3 \cdot analyst, 3 \cdot assistant>, <group \to 1 \cdot analyst, 3 \cdot assistant>\},$$

(URs are represented in angle brackets for unambiguity). These UMGs define, respectively, following sets of terminal multisets:

$$\overline{V}_{S_{0,2}} = \{\{6 \cdot analyst, 4 \cdot assistant\}, \{4 \cdot assistant\}\},$$
$$\overline{V}_{S_{0,3}} = \{\{6 \cdot analyst, 6 \cdot assistant\}, \{6 \cdot assistant\}\},$$
$$\overline{V}_{S_{1,2}} = \{\{7 \cdot analyst, 4 \cdot assistant\}, \{3 \cdot analyst, 4 \cdot assistant\}\},$$
$$\overline{V}_{S_{1,3}} = \{\{7 \cdot analyst, 6 \cdot assistant\}, \{3 \cdot analyst, 6 \cdot assistant\}\},$$
$$\overline{V}_{S} = \left(\overline{V}_{S_{0,2}} \cup \overline{V}_{S_{0,3}} \cup \overline{V}_{S_{1,2}} \cup \overline{V}_{S_{1,3}}\right) \downarrow \{2 \le analyst \le 6\}) \downarrow \{assistant = \min\}$$
$$= \{6 \cdot analyst, 4 \cdot assistant\}, \{6 \cdot analyst, 6 \cdot assistant\}, \{6 \cdot assistant\},$$
$$\{3 \cdot analyst, 4 \cdot assistant\}, \{3 \cdot analyst, 6 \cdot assistant\} \downarrow \{assistant = \min\}$$
$$= \{\{6 \cdot analyst, 4 \cdot assistant\}, \{3 \cdot analyst, 4 \cdot assistant\}\}. \quad \blacksquare$$

As may be seen, Eqs. (64)–(66) define boundary conditions, concerning objects and variables, and optimizing conditions, concerning only objects, that is why from both theoretical and practical points of view, it is reasonable to extend UMMG filters by optimizing conditions, relating variables. By analogy with Eq. (65), such conditions will have the form:

$$\gamma = opt. \tag{77}$$

This form defines optimality of the generated terminal multisets through multiplicity-variable values, used while these TMS generation. Eq. (77) semantics is quite clear: select those TMS, which are generated by the help of value of variable γ, which (value) is minimal (maximal) among all other TMS, generated by γ application. As seen, Eq. (77) extends optimality definition from only multiplicities-constants, having places in TMS, to also multiplicities-variables, having places in unitary metarules, applied while TMS generation.

Most simple formal definition of the verbally described sense of Eq. (77) optimizing condition may be as follows. Let us introduce l auxiliary terminal objects $\overline{\gamma}_1, ..., \overline{\gamma}_l$ corresponding variables $\gamma_1, ..., \gamma_l$, having places in UMMG $S = \langle a_0, R, F \rangle$, i.e., unitary metarules and boundary condition (66). After that, let us add one new unitary metarule:

$$a_0' \rightarrow 1 \cdot a_0, \gamma_1 \cdot \overline{\gamma}_1, \dots, \gamma_k \cdot \overline{\gamma}_l \qquad (78)$$

to scheme R, thus creating scheme R', which contains Eq. (78) and all elements of R, and substituting all optimizing conditions of the form $\gamma = opt$ by $\overline{\gamma} = opt$ in filter F, thus converting them to the "canonical" form (65)—remember, $\overline{\gamma}$ is object not variable and, more, terminal object, because there is no any UR or UMR with head $\overline{\gamma}$ in R. Obtained filter will be denoted as F'.

As seen now, UMMG $S' = \langle a_0', R', F' \rangle$ generates terminal multisets of the form:

$$\{n_{i_1} \cdot a_{i_1}, \dots, n_{i_k} \cdot a_{i_k}, \overline{n}_1 \cdot \overline{\gamma}_1, \dots, \overline{n}_l \cdot \overline{\gamma}_l\}, \qquad (79)$$

where

$$\{n_{i_1} \cdot a_{i_1}, \dots, n_{i_l} \cdot a_{i_l}\} \in \overline{V}_S, \qquad (80)$$

and TMS (79) will be selected to $\overline{V}_{S'}$, if and only if TMS (80) satisfies all conditions, entering F and concerning terminal objects $a_{i_1}, \dots, a_{i_k}$, as well as TMS $\{\overline{n}_1 \cdot \overline{\gamma}_1, \dots, \overline{n}_l \cdot \overline{\gamma}_l\}$ satisfies all optimizing conditions of the form $\overline{\gamma}_i = opt \in F'$, corresponding $\gamma_i = opt \in F$..

It is not difficult to define $\overline{V}_S$ by subtracting from all $v' \in \overline{V}_{S'}$ multisets of the form $\{\overline{n}_1 \cdot \overline{\gamma}_1, \dots, \overline{n}_l \cdot \overline{\gamma}_l\}$, but from the practical point of view, it is more useful to consider not $\overline{V}_S$ but $\overline{V}_{S'}$ as a result of application of unitary multimetagrammar S: it is clear that all $v' \in \overline{V}_{S'}$ contain values $\overline{n}_1, \dots, \overline{n}_l$ of variables $\gamma_1, \dots, \gamma_l$ as terminal objects $\overline{\gamma}_1, \dots, \overline{\gamma}_l$ multiplicities, which computation is often main purpose of the mentioned application.

Example 8. As may be seen, problem, described in Section 2, is to obtain m quantity of laboratories, as well as n and l quantities of analysts and assistants, respectively, in one laboratory. Although Eqs. (18)–(20) do not contain optimizing conditions of the form $\gamma = opt$, generating TMS like

$$\{100 \cdot employee, 115000 \cdot eur, 3 \cdot m, 2 \cdot n, 5 \cdot l\} \qquad (81)$$

is much more useful than TMS like {100·*employee*, 115,000·*eur*} because of Eq. (81) with greater informativity (here, we use m, n, l instead of $\overline{n}, \overline{m}, \overline{l}$). ∎

So we shall use $\overline{V}_{S'}$ as a result of $S = \langle a_0, R, F \rangle$ unitary multimetagrammar application, even if R does not include variable-containing optimizing conditions.

To finish with syntax and semantics of UMGs/UMMGs, let us note that class of unitary multigrammars is strict subclass of filtering unitary multiset grammars (UMGs ⊂ FUMGs): every UMGs is FUMGs with empty filter. From the other side, FUMGs are strict subclass of unitary multiset metagrammars (UMGs ⊂ FUMGs): every FUMGs is UMMGs without variable multiplicities and corresponding variable declarations inside filter.

UMG/UMMG algorithmics and applications are considered in the separate chapter of this book.

Author details

Igor Sheremet
Financial University under the Government of Russian Federation, Moscow, Russia

*Address all correspondence to: sheremet@rfbr.ru

References

[1] Whitten JL, Bentley LD. Introduction to Systems Analysis and Design. New York: McGraw-Hill Irwin; 2006. p. 640

[2] Bentley LD, Whitten JL. Systems Analysis and Design for the Global Enterprise. New York: McGraw-Hill Irwin; 2007. p. 160

[3] Blanchard BS, Fabrycky WJ. Systems Engineering and Analysis. Englewood Cliffs, NJ: Prentice-Hall; 2010. p. 723

[4] Lasdon SL. Optimization Theory for Large Systems. NY: Dover Publications; 2013. p. 560

[5] Tilly S, Rosenblatt HJ. System Analysis and Design. Boston, MA: Cengage Learning; Ebook-dl.com. 2016. p. 572

[6] Sainter P, Oldham K, Larkin A, Murton A, Brimble R. Product knowledge management within knowledge-based engineering system. – In: Proceedings of ASME 2000 Design Engineering Technical Conference. – Baltimore, Maryland: ASME, 2000. pp. 1-8

[7] Akerkar R, Sajja P. Knowledge-Based Systems. Sudbury, MA: Jones and Bartlett Publishers; 2010. p. 350

[8] Kendal SL, Green M. An Introduction to Knowledge Engineering. London: Springer; 2007. p. 300

[9] Pannu A. Artificial intelligence and its application in different areas. International Journal of Engineering and Innovative Technology. 2015;**4**(4):79-84

[10] Cross TB. The Uses of Artificial Intelligence in Business. New York: Prentice Hall; TECHtionary.com. 2017. p. 271

[11] Gass SI, Assad AA. An Annotated Timeline of Operations Research: An Informal History. NY: Kluwer Academic Publishers; 2005. p. 213

[12] Franks B. The Analytics Revolution: How to Improve Your Business by Making Analytics Operational in the Big Data Era. New York: John Wiley & Sons; 2014. p. 307

[13] Hillier SF, Lieberman GJ. Introduction to Operations Research. Boston, MA: McGraw Hill; 2014. p. 1237

[14] Taha HA. Operations Research: An Introduction. London: Pearson; 2016. p. 838

[15] Marriott K, Stucky PG. Programming with Constraints: An Introduction. Cambridge, MA: MIT Press; 2003. p. 420

[16] Apt K. Principles of Constraint Programming. Cambridge, UK: Cambridge University Press; 2003. p. 420

[17] Frunkwirth T, Abdennadher S. Essentials of Constraint Programming. Berlin: Springer Verlag; 2003. p. 398

[18] Lake J. Sets, fuzzy sets, multisets and functions. Journal of the London Mathematical Society. 1976;**12**:323-326

[19] Hickman JL. A note on the concept of multiset. Bulletin of the Australian Mathematical Society. 1980;**22**:211-217. DOI: 10.1017/S000497270000650X

[20] Meyer RK, McRobbie MA. Multisets and relevant implication. I, II. Australasian Journal of Philosophy. 1982;**60**:107-139. DOI: 10.1080/00048408212340551

[21] Banatre J-P, Le Metayer D. Programming by multiset

transformation. Communications of the ACM. 1993;**36**:98-111. DOI: 10.1145/151233.151242

[22] Marriott K. Constraint multiset grammars. In: Proceedings of IEEE Symposium on Visual Languages. IEEE Computer Society Press; 1994. pp. 118-125. DOI: 10.1109/VL.1994.363633

[23] Marriott K. Parsing visual languages with constraint multiset grammars. In: Programming Languages: Implementation, Logic and Programs. Lecture Notes in Computer Science. Vol. 1292. New York: Springer; 1996. p. 419

[24] Marriott K, Meyer B. On the classification of visual languages by grammar hierarchies. Journal of Visual Languages and Computing. 1997;**8**: 375-402. DOI: 10.1006/jvlc.1997.0053

[25] Calude CS, Paun G, Rozenberg G, Salomaa A. Multisets Processing: Mathematical, Computer Science and Molecular Computing Points of View. Lecture Notes in Computer Science. Vol. 2235. NY: Springer; 2001. p. 359. DOI: 10.1007/3-540-45523-X

[26] Petrovsky AB. Main Notions of the Multisets Theory. Moscow: URSS; 2002. p. 80. (In Russian)

[27] Petrovsky AB. Sets and Multisets Spaces. Moscow: URSS; 2003. p. 248. (In Russian)

[28] Singh D, Ibrahim AM, Yohanna T, Singh JN. An overview of applications of multisets. Novi Sad Journal of Mathematics. 2007;**37**:37-92

[29] Red'ko VN, Bui DB, Grishko Yu A. Modern state of multisets theory from the entity point of view. Cybernetics and Systems Analysis. 2015;**51**:171-178

[30] Sheremet I. A. Recursive Multisets and Their Applications. – Moscow: Nauka; 2010. p. 293. (In Russian)

[31] Sheremet IA. Recursive Multisets and Their Applications. Berlin: NG Verlag; 2011. p. 249

[32] Chomsky N. Syntactic Structures. The Hague: Mouton de Gruyter; 2002. p. 118

[33] Meduna A. Formal Languages and Computation: Models and their Application. New York: CRC Press; 2014. p. 233

[34] Wallace M. Constraint logic programming. In: Computational Logic: Logic Programming and Beyond. Lecture Notes in Computer Science. New York: Springer; Vol. 2407. 2002. pp. 512-556

[35] Bratko I. Prolog Programming for Artificial Intelligence. NY: Addison-Wesley; 2012. p. 696

[36] Diaz D. GNU Prolog. www.gprolog.org. 2018. p. 238

Chapter 6

Unitary Multiset Grammars an Metagrammars Algorithmics and Application

Igor Sheremet

Abstract

The chapter is dedicated to the algorithmics of unitary multiset grammars and metagrammars. Their application to some actual problems from the area of large-scale sociotechnical systems (STS) assessment and optimization is also considered: estimation of capabilities of the producing STS; amounts of resources, necessary to such STS for various orders completion; assessment of STS sustainability/vulnerability to various destructive impacts (natural disasters, technogenic catastrophes, mutual sanctions, etc.); and STS profit maximization, as well as works optimal distribution among non-antagonistic competing STS, operating in the market economy.

Keywords: systems analysis, operations research, knowledge engineering, digital economy, multisets recursive multisets, multiset grammars, unitary multiset grammars and multimetagrammars, sociotechnical systems assessment and optimization

1. Introduction

Unitary multiset grammars (UMG) and multimetagrammars (UMMG) are knowledge representation model, providing convergence of classical operations research and modern knowledge engineering. The main area of UMG/UMMG application is assessment and optimization of large-scale sociotechnical systems (STS). Syntax and semantics of multigrammars are described in the first part of this work, being separate chapter of this book. Section 2 of this chapter contains primary description of UMG/UMMG-improved algorithmics, providing generation of terminal multisets (TMS), reduced by unperspective branches cutoff at the maximal early steps of generation. Such branches do not lead to the TMS, satisfying all conditions, entering filter of UMG/UMMG. Section 3 is dedicated to UMG/UMMG application to some actual problems from the STS assessment area (estimation of producing STS capabilities and resources, necessary to such systems for various orders completion, as well as assessment of STS sustainability and vulnerability to various destructive impacts, such as natural disasters, technogenic catastrophes, mutual sanctions, etc.). In Section 4, optimization problems, related to STS, are considered (their profit maximization and works' optimal distribution among non-antagonistic competing STS in the market economy). Conclusion contains list of directions of further development of multigrammatical approach.

2. Algorithmics of unitary multigrammars and multimetagrammars

Let us begin from **filtering unitary multigrammars** (FUMG).

From the computational complexity point of view, definition (58) from the first part of this work may be without loss of generated TMS transformed to

$$V_{(i+1)} = V_{(i)} \cup \left(\bigcup_{\substack{v \in V_{(i)} \\ \langle a \rightarrow n_1 \cdot a_1, \cdots, n_m \cdot a_m \rangle \in R}} \bigcup_{n \cdot a \exists \in v} \{v - \{n \cdot a\} + n * \{n_1 \cdot a_1, \cdots, n_m \cdot a_m\}\} \right) \quad (1)$$

where $\exists \in$ means selection of any one multiobject $n \cdot a$ from the multiset v instead of repeating such selection for all multiobjects $n \cdot a \in v$. This provides essential reduction of the computational complexity of TMS generation [1] and is basic for all algorithms, described lower in this section.

As may be seen, sufficiently valuable part of multisets, generated by FUMG unitary rules (UR) application, may be eliminated after few generation steps, because all the following steps do not lead to TMS, satisfying FUMG filter boundary conditions, or have no opportunity for further optimization over terminal multisets, generated earlier, if concerning optimizing conditions. So essence of general approach, which is described further, is to apply filter to every new generated multiset (not only terminal) and to cut off those multisets, which are not perspective in the aforementioned sense. Thus we apply well known and widely used in operations research "branches and bounds" scheme to TMS generation. Of course, filter application to generated nonterminal multisets cannot be identical to filter application to terminal multisets; that is why some additional considerations are necessary.

Let us take the definition of TMS generation logic (57)–(61) from the first part of the work as a basis and construct rather simple and transparent procedure-function terminal multisets generation (*TMSG*), providing reduced generation of set of terminal multisets, defined by FUMG.

We shall use the following variables in the *TMSG* body:

1. v, which value is current generated multiset.

2. R, which value is set of unitary rules (FUMG scheme), applied to multisets in order to generate new multisets.

3. F, which value is FUMG filter used for selection of terminal multisets to the resulting set V.

4. V, accumulating terminal multisets, satisfying filter F, while generation.

5. FT, which value is set of triples *<a, opt, l>*, each corresponding to optimizing condition $a = opt \in F$, where a is object, $opt \in \{\max, \min\}$, and l is current value of object a multiplicity obtained after previous generation steps.

6. Couples *<a, w>* and *<a, c>*, which are representations of unitary rule $a \leftarrow n_1 \cdot a_1, ..., n_m \cdot a_m$, where w as well as c is multiset $\{n_1 \cdot a_1, ..., n_m \cdot a_m\}$.

In *TMSG* body, F, FT, and V are global variables, which are available from all subfunction calls while generation is executed. Note F is read-only variable, while V and FT are updated (read-write) variables. All other variables are local and are used in the area of their functions in such a way that every new function call operates its own values of these variables.

```
TMSG body is the following:
TMSG: procedure (v, R, F) returns (V);
        variables F, V, FT global; variables v, R local;
        v := {∅}; FT := {∅};
        /* initial values of optimized multiplicities settings */
        do a = opt ∈ F;
        case opt:
              {min : if k ≤ a ≤ k' ∈ F
                        then FT : ∪ {⟨a, min, k'⟩};
                        else FT : ∪ {⟨a, min, MAX⟩};
               max : if k ≤ a ≤ k' ∈ F
                        then FT : ∪ {⟨a, max, k⟩};
                        else FT : ∪ {⟨a, max, 0⟩};
              };
        end F;
        /*main part: generation function G call */
        call G(v, R);
        /*function G body*/
        G: procedure (v, R);
           if v is terminal multiset
             then {call FILTER(v);
               return;};
        /*v is non-terminal multiset, and following operators provide selection of
        unperspective multisets and redundant generation cut-off */
        do n · a ∈ v where a is terminal object;
          if k ≤ a ≤ k' ∈ F & n>k' /* n already exceeds higher bound */
             then return;
          if ⟨a, min, l⟩ ∈ FT
             then if l<n /* current minimized multiplicity of object a is already
             lower than n, which cannot decrease */
                     then return;
        end v;
        /* branch is perspective, so new multisets are generated */
        select n · a∃ ∈ v where a is non-terminal object;
        do ⟨a, w⟩ ∈ R ; /* all non-terminal object a alternatives */
           call G(v − {n · a} + n∗w, R);
        end aw;
        end;
end G;
FILTER: procedure (v); /* generated TMS v filtration */
variables v, x local;
        do n · a ∈ v ;
          if k ≤ a ≤ k' ∈ F
             then if (n < k)∨(n>k') /* n is out of [k, k'] */
                     then return;
          if ⟨a, min, l⟩ ∈ FT
             then if l<n /* n is greater than already stored min value */
                     then return;
          if ⟨a, max, l⟩ ∈ FT
             then if l>n /* n is less than already stored max value */
```

```
                    then return;
        end na;
        /* correction min/max values by new terminal multiset*/
        x := 0; /* flag "no values corrected" */
        do ⟨a, opt, l⟩ ∈ FT
            do n · a ∈ v ;
                if l ≠ n /* at least one value corrected */
                    then {FT : −{⟨a, opt, l⟩} ∪ {⟨a, opt, n⟩}; /*replacement*/x := 1};
                    /*flag reset*/
            end na;
        end opt;
        if x=0 /* no values corrected */
            then V : ∪ {v}; /* one more TMS added to the accumulated set */
            else V := {v}; /* replacement of earlier accumulated set */
        end FILTER;
    end TMSG
```

Let us comment on the represented procedure-function *TMSG*.

As seen, it contains prefix, which provides *V* and *FT* variable values initialization. *FT* value is set of triples, each corresponding to one optimizing condition, entering filter *F*. If there is boundary condition $k \le a \le k' \in F,$ then initial value of object a multiplicity would be k' in the case condition is $a = \min$, and k otherwise. Both values correspond to the worst cases. If there is not any boundary condition with the same object a, where $a = opt \in F$, then, obviously, the worst case for $a = \min$ is MAX (the largest possible multiplicity for the considered problem), while for $a = \max$, it is 0. After prefix execution, there is unique operation, returning result of recursive procedure *G* call with input values v and *R,* passed without any changes from *TMSG* call itself.

Procedure *G* is core of the described algorithm; it implements the main part of generation and consists of three sections.

First section corresponds to that case, when v is terminal multiset, and all that is necessary here is to apply FUMG filter to v, what is really done by procedure *FILTER* call with v input data. After this call, processing of TMS v is terminated.

If v is not terminal multiset, it is clear that v contains one or more nonterminal objects, which may be used for generation continuation. The last is performed by the second section of *G* in such a way that multiset v is checked, where it is perspective in the above sense or it may be eliminated from generation, because all TMS, generated from v, would not satisfy *F*. For this purpose, all terminal multiobjects are checked by two selection criteria:

1. If in terminal multiobject $n \cdot a$ multiplicity n already exceeds upper bound k′ of boundary condition $k \le a \le k' \in F$. (it's obvious that while following generation steps, object a multiplicity would only increase or in the utmost case remain unchangeable).

2. If mentioned multiplicity is greater than value l already having place in the triple $\langle a, \min, l \rangle \in FT$ (again it's obvious that the following steps would not decrease this multiplicity, so all TMS generated from *V* would not satisfy optimizing filter $a = \min$).

(There may be more sophisticated and efficient criteria for earlier recognition and cutting off unperspective generation branches [2, 3], but chapter volume limits make their description impossible). If one of the checked conditions is not satisfied, further generation from multiset v is terminated by return from *G* without any operation.

The third section of G corresponds to nonterminal multiset, which was not eliminated, being perspective, so generation is continued by all possible branches, corresponding to unitary rules with the same head, in full accordance with UMG semantics and improvement (1), by G recursive calls with new input data.

Function *FILTER* with unique input (multiset v) implements check of all conditions, having place in filter F. This is done by the first **do-end** loop for all terminal multiobjects, entering v. If one of these checks failed, return from *FILTER* is performed without any additional actions. If all checks were successful, second section is executed. It begins from the installation of flag variable x to 0 value; that means no min/max values in the accumulating variable FT were replaced (i.e., v has no multiobjects $n \cdot a$ with value n more or less over already having place in FT). After that, **do-end** loop for all FT elements is executed. If multiplicity n of object a in TMS v is not equal to value l in the considered element $\langle a, opt, l \rangle \in FT$; that means n is less (when $opt = \min$) or greater (when $opt = \max$) than l, so l must be replaced by n, and flag x must get value 1 (at least one replacement was done). The third section of function *FILTER* operates according to variable x value. If $x = 0$ (i.e., all optimized multiplicities in v are equal to already obtained in the previous generation steps), then v is joined to the resulting set V as new element. If $x = 1$ (i.e., at least one multiplicity was replaced, so v is "better" than earlier created and stored terminal multisets), then previous value of V is replaced by one-element set $\{v\}$.

As seen, the described algorithm due to its simplicity may be implemented easily on every available software/hardware environment. Correctness of this algorithm is confirmed by the following statement [2, 3].

Statement. Let $S = \langle a_0, R, F \rangle$, and *TMSG* $(\{1 \cdot a_0\}, R, F)$ is result of *TMSG* call. Then

$$TMSG(\{1 \cdot a_0\}, R, F) = \overline{V}_S. \quad \blacksquare \tag{2}$$

(Note *TMSG* operates only elementary boundary conditions $a\rho n$, not EBC $a\rho a'$, neither CBC. *TMSG* generalization is not associated with any difficulties).

Let us describe now the main idea of **algorithmics of generation sets of TMS, defined by unitary multimetagrammars**.

As shown in [2, 3], all multisets, generated by any UMMG, have form

$$v = \left\{C_{a_{i_1}} \cdot a_{i_1}, \dots, C_{a_{i_m}} \cdot a_{i_m}\right\}, \tag{3}$$

where every $C_{a_{i_j}}$ is so-called variables-containing multiplicity (VCM), being polynom of variables-multiplicities, having places in unitary metarules, used while generation of multiset v. In the general case, object a VCM is

$$C_a = n_i^a + \sum_{i=1}^{N_{C_a}} n_i^a \cdot \left(\gamma_1^i\right)^{l_{i_1}^a} \cdot \dots \cdot \left(\gamma_{m_i}^i\right)^{l_{im_i}^a}, \tag{4}$$

where N_{C_a} is number of monoms, each being product of all occurrences of variables-multiplicities and constants-multiplicities, having places in one generation branch, leading to object a.

If filter F of UMMG contains boundary conditions

$$\begin{aligned} k_1 \le a_{i_1} \le k_1', \\ \dots. \\ k_l \le a_{i_l} \le k_l' \end{aligned} \tag{5}$$

as well as optimizing conditions

$$a_{j_1} = opt_1,$$
$$\dots\qquad (6)$$
$$a_{j_t} = opt_t,$$

they induce l inequalities

$$k_1 \le C_{a_{i_1}} \le k'_1,$$
$$\dots\qquad (7)$$
$$k_l \le C_{a_{i_l}} \le k'_l,$$

and t goal functions

$$C_{a_{j_1}} \to opt_{j_1},$$
$$\dots\qquad (8)$$
$$C_{a_{j_t}} \to opt_{j_t}.$$

Domain of every variable γ, having place in polynoms $C_{a_{i_1}}, \dots, C_{a_{i_l}}, C_{j_1}, \dots, C_{j_t}$, is defined by boundary condition

$$k_\gamma \le \gamma \le k'_\gamma \in F. \qquad (9)$$

As seen from (3)–(9), set of terminal multisets, generated in the UMMG case, corresponds to set of solutions of multicriterial problem of discrete polynomial programming. There are well-known approaches to such problems' consideration [4, 5], but their common feature is they provide search of any one of the solutions, not all multi-element solutions set, if it exists. Proposed UMMG TMS generation algorithmics [2, 3] is initially oriented to UMMG semantic precise implementation and combines mixed computation and interval analysis techniques [6–9] with global optimization based on theory [10–13]. Aforementioned algorithmics provides multidirectional reduction of redundant generation branches by procedure, similar to *TMSG*, and extended by splitting of intervals, defined by boundary conditions, which describe variable domains, to subintervals, until the last become points. Every such step is accompanied by the estimation of lower and upper bounds of VCMs, containing variable, which current domain is splitted, so if both bounds of at least one VCM are out of interval, defined by corresponding object multiplicity bounds, having place in UMMG filter, then created interval is eliminated, and generation branch is terminated.

As *TMSG*, another powerful tool of unperspective branches early recognition and cutoff is comparison of mentioned lower and upper bound estimates with already obtained values of optimized multiplicities. If corresponding optimizing condition is a = min, and current value of object a multiplicity, obtained as a result of previous steps execution, is n, then when lower bound estimate of VCM of a is $\overline{n}$, and already $\overline{n}>n$, so further generation by this branch, which leads only to growth of VCM (or it remains unchangeable in the best case), is senseless, and branch may be terminated. Similarly, if optimizing condition is a = max, and current value of corresponding multiplicity is n, while VCM upper bound estimate is $\overline{n}' < n$, then further generation by this branch will not lead to object a multiplicity increase, and branch may be terminated.

VCM generation is based on unified representation of polynoms in (4) form as sets of multisets: C_a is represented as

$$v_a = \left\{ \{n_0^a \cdot \overline{\gamma}_0\}, \left\{n_1^a \cdot \overline{\gamma}_0, e_{1_1}^a \cdot \overline{\gamma}_1^1, \dots, e_{1_{m_1}}^a \cdot \overline{\gamma}_{m_1}^1 \right\}, \dots, \left\{n_k^a \cdot \overline{\gamma}_0, e_{k_1}^a \cdot \overline{\gamma}_1^k, \dots, e_{k_{m_k}}^a \cdot \overline{\gamma}_{m_k}^k \right\} \right\}, \tag{10}$$

where $k = N_{C_a}$, $\overline{\gamma}_j^i$ are objects, corresponding to variables, while $\overline{\gamma}_0$ is fictive object, corresponding to constants, having place in polynom. For example, polynom

$$C_a = 5 + 3 \cdot (\gamma_1)^2 \cdot (\gamma_2)^4 + (\gamma_2)^5 \cdot \gamma_3 \tag{11}$$

is represented by multiset

$$v_a = \{\{5 \cdot \overline{\gamma}_0\}, \{3 \cdot \overline{\gamma}_0, 2 \cdot \overline{\gamma}_1, 4 \cdot \overline{\gamma}_3\}, \{1 \cdot \overline{\gamma}_0, 5 \cdot \overline{\gamma}_2, 1 \cdot \overline{\gamma}_3\}\}. \tag{12}$$

This representation is sufficiently flexible, and it is the basis of implementation of mixed computation in the multisets case; the core of this implementation is polynoms multiplication and addition.

More detailed description of algorithmics, providing efficient generation of sets of terminal multisets, defined by unitary multimetagrammars, needs separate survey.

Implementation issues, related with the proposed knowledge representation model, are described in [1, 14].

However, presented formal definitions of syntax, semantics, and algorithmics of UMG/UMMG are, in our opinion, sufficient for consideration of their pragmatics, that is, their application to various practical problems.

3. Assessment of the producing sociotechnical systems

Multigrammatical paradigm and UMG/UMMG toolkit are sufficiently general and simple to formalize and solve a lot of practical problems from various areas of operations research and systems analysis. Techniques, shortly described in Section 2 of the first part of this work, is one of the many possible to apply. Some more examples from hierarchical sociotechnical systems assessment and design concerned reader may find in [2, 3], where one may find also description of multigrammatical emulation of well-known classical problems of optimization theory: shortest path, traveling salesman, maximal flow, maximal pair matching, optimal assignments problems, and transport problem as well as integer linear programming problem. (Note that in [2, 3], there is also analysis of interconnections between multigrammars' family and known computational models, such as Petri nets, vectors addition, substitution systems, etc.).

Lower in this section, we shall consider problems, associated with the producing (manufacturing) STS, being most complicated for modeling.

Let us introduce the following **structural interpretation of unitary rules**.

We shall understand UR

$$a \to n_1 \cdot a_1, \dots, n_m \cdot a_m \tag{13}$$

as follows: object a consists of n_1 objects a_1, ..., n_m objects a_m .

In turn, **technological interpretation of unitary rules** is generalization of the structural one and is as follows: production of one object (unit of resource) a requires n_1 objects (units of resource) a_1, ..., n_m objects (units of resource) a_m. One may consider (13) as a black box, representing producing device or manufacturing facility (factory, plant, etc.), containing a lot of such devices, working cooperatively. Set R of such URs represents technological base (TB) of some social group, possessing represented by this set producing (manufacturing) equipment. If R contains $l > 1$ URs with identical head and different bodies, this means that one and the same object may be produced in l various ways (by l various devices, or by one and the same device, but by various methods, or by l various facilities). Objects, having places in URs, may be manufactured devices, their blocks, spare parts, chips, pieces of connecting cables, various measured resources involved (necessary amounts of electrical energy, liquids, solid materials, etc. "down to ore"), as well as time and money. Manufactured devices may be, in turn, manufacturing ("means of production") and may be used further in production processes/chains.

Unitary multigrammars provide most natural "top-down" way of formal description of technological base of arbitrary producing STS, as well as deep structure of manufactured objects of any level of structural complexity (obviously, these two entities are interconnected closely). "Additivity" of multigrammatical knowledge bases (KB), being consequence of their "granularity" (due to unitary rules and metarules as knowledge representation atoms), provides creating and updating KB in near real time. Since now we shall use notations "multigrammatical knowledge base" and "scheme of UMG/UMMG" as synonyms.

Example 1. Consider car, consisting of body, engine, transmission, four wheels, and fuel cistern. Car body, in turn, consists of frame, front and back glasses, engine cover, baggage place, and two first and two second doors. Engine includes motor, cooling system, and accumulator. All the said may be represented by the following set of unitary rules in the structural interpretation:

$$\begin{aligned}
&car \to 1 \cdot body, 1 \cdot engine, 1 \cdot transmission, 4 \cdot wheel, 1 \cdot fuel\text{-}cisterm,\\
&body \to 1 \cdot frame, 1 \cdot front\text{-}glass, 1 \cdot back\text{-}glass, 1 \cdot engine\text{-}cover, 1 \cdot baggage\text{-}place,\\
&\qquad 2 \cdot first\text{-}door, 2 \cdot back\text{-}door,\\
&engine \to 1 \cdot motor, 1 \cdot cooling\text{-}system, 1 \cdot accumulator. \quad \blacksquare
\end{aligned}$$

As it is easy to see, all terminal objects may become nonterminal after joining to this set of new URs, detailing them down to undivided spare parts. If to follow technological interpretation, then every UR reflects assembling operation, implemented by corresponding segment of manufacturing facility: one such segment is assembling car of the listed components, another segment - body, etc.

To take into account cost of any operation executed (obviously, it is "*added value*" *in K. Marx terminology*), as well as time interval necessary for its execution, it is sufficient to include to UR bodies multiobjects like $n \cdot e$ and $m \cdot t$, where e and t are fixed-name objects being cost and time measurement units (e.g., *usd* and *sec*). There may be recalculation of both to another unit by including to the KB additional rules, reflecting currencies interrelations and different time scales, for example,

$$eur \to 1.15 \cdot usd, \tag{14}$$

$$hour \to 60 \cdot mnt, \tag{15}$$

$$mnt \to 60 \cdot sec \tag{16}$$

(rational multiplicities' appearance along with integer ones, considered higher, does not bring any principal transformations and difficulties into MG semantics and algorithmics [2, 3]). Both cost and time may be defined in "compound" units, that is, UR body may contain three multiobjects, $3 \cdot hour$, $23 \cdot \min$, $15 \cdot \sec$, that after application of URs (14)–(16) will be transformed to one multiobject, $10953 \cdot \sec$.

Considering time intervals description in unitary rules, we must take into account that, unlike cost, time is not fully additive resource, because producing devices may operate in parallel. That's why time is additive resource only regarding separate device, and typical form of "local time" description is multiobject $n \cdot \langle t - x \rangle$, where x may be manufacturing device name as well as assembled technical object name, while t is time measurement unit (here angle brackets are used for syntactical unambiguity).

Example 2. Let us consider the following cost and time parameters, implanted to URs from example 1. Let cost of one car assembling is 3000 USD; body, 2000 USD; and engine, 6000 USD; time interval necessary for one car assembling is 28 minutes, body, 21 minutes; and engine, 63 minutes. Then URs from Example 1 may be rewritten in the following way:

$$\begin{aligned}
&car \to 28 \cdot \langle mnt - car \rangle, 3000 \cdot usd, 1 \cdot body, 1 \cdot engine, 1 \cdot transmission, 4 \cdot wheel,\\
&\quad 1 \cdot fuel\text{-}cisterm,\\
&body \to 21 \cdot \langle mnt - body \rangle, 2000 \cdot usd, 1 \cdot front\text{-}glass, 1 \cdot back\text{-}glass, 1 \cdot engine\text{-}cover, 1 \cdot baggage\text{-}place,\\
&\quad 2 \cdot first\text{-}door, 2 \cdot back\text{-}door,\\
&engine \to 60 \cdot \langle mnt - engine \rangle, 6000 \cdot usd, 1 \cdot motor, 1 \cdot cooling\text{-}system, 1 \cdot accumulator. \quad \blacksquare
\end{aligned}$$

If we have knowledge base, prepared as shown above, then it may be used to estimate resources amounts, necessary to complete any order by means of technological base, defined by R. Order may be represented as multiset

$$q = \{m_1 \cdot b_1, ..., m_k \cdot b_k\}, \tag{17}$$

which means customer needs m_1 objects b_1, ..., m_k objects b_k.

Then, as it is easy to see, resources collection, necessary to complete this order, is terminal multiset $\overline{v}$ being element of set of TMS $\overline{V}_{S_q}$, where

$$S_q = \langle a_q, R_q \rangle, \tag{18}$$

$$R_q = R \cup \{\langle a_q \to m_1 \cdot b_1, ..., m_k \cdot b_k \rangle\} \tag{19}$$

(unitary rule, having place in (19), is in angle brackets for unambiguity). If unitary multigrammar S_q generates one-element SMS, that is, $|\overline{V}_{S_q}| = 1$, there is unique variant of aforementioned resources collection. Otherwise, $|\overline{V}_{S_q}| > 1$, and there are various ways of some objects' assembling, each consuming its own resources collection.

Example 3. Let $q = \{3 \cdot car\}$. Then R_q consists of all URs from Example 2 and unitary rule

$$order \to 3 \cdot car, \tag{20}$$

that is, order is to assemble three cars. According to (17)–(19),

$$\begin{aligned}
\overline{V}_{S_q} = \{\{&84 \cdot \langle mnt\text{-}car \rangle, 63 \cdot \langle mnt\text{-}body \rangle, 180 \cdot \langle mnt\text{-}engine \rangle, 27000 \cdot usd,\\
&3 \cdot transmission, 12 \cdot wheel, 3 \cdot fuel\text{-}cistern, 3 \cdot front\text{-}glass, 3 \cdot back\text{-}glass,\\
&3 \cdot engine\text{-}\mathrm{cover}, 3 \cdot baggage\text{-}\mathrm{place}, 6 \cdot \mathrm{first\text{-}door}, 6 \cdot \mathrm{back\text{-}door},\\
&3 \cdot motor, 3 \cdot cooling\text{-}system, 3 \cdot accumulator\}\}.
\end{aligned}$$

That means order completion requires spare parts from external suppliers as well as money and time for assembling segments of manufacturing facility in amounts, being multiplicities of corresponding objects, having places in $\overline{V}_{S_q}$. There is the only one variant of resources set necessary for order completion. ■

If it is necessary to evaluate (estimate) total cost of order completion, then it is sufficient to join to the KB R unitary rules, defining costs of all necessary spare parts and other external ("outsourced") resources. These URs may have form $a \rightarrow n \cdot e$, where a is terminal object from R, while e is monetary unit, used for cost calculation. As may be seen, if one would eliminate from URs time-defining multiobjects, then e becomes unique terminal object of the created scheme R', and set of terminal multisets generated by UMG $S' = \left\langle a_q, R'_q \right\rangle$ would contain one-element TMS of form $\{\overline{n} \cdot e\}$, where $\overline{n}$ is total cost of order completion, corresponding to one of its variants (as was said higher, there may be more than one such variant).

Example 4. Let us add to the KB from Example 3 the following unitary rules, defining prices of car the outsourced elements:

$$
\begin{aligned}
&\textit{transmission} \rightarrow 100 \cdot \textit{usd},\\
&\textit{wheel} \qquad\quad \rightarrow 50 \cdot \textit{usd},\\
&\qquad\qquad\quad \ldots\\
&\textit{accumulator} \rightarrow 10 \cdot \textit{usd}.
\end{aligned}
$$

As seen, new UMG provides generation of one-element set

$$\{\{84 \cdot \langle \textit{mnt-car} \rangle, 63 \cdot \langle \textit{mnt-body} \rangle, 180 \cdot \langle \textit{mnt-engine} \rangle, X \cdot \textit{usd}\}\},$$

where X is total cost of order completion, that is, three car assembling.

If multiobjects $28 \cdot \langle \textit{mnt-car} \rangle$, $21 \cdot \langle \textit{mnt-body} \rangle$ and $60 \cdot \langle \textit{mnt-engine} \rangle$ are eliminated from UR set presented in Example 10, then obtained UMG will generate one-element set $\{\{X \cdot \textit{usd}\}\}$. ■

In practice every STS, which is capable to complete input orders and manufacture some output production, possesses usually not only technological base but also resource base (RB). For this reason, **assessment of STS capability to orders completion** requires comparison of two resources collections—being in system's ownership and necessary. In multigrammatical paradigm, this problem is solved quite simply.

Let R be technological base, while multiset $\overline{v} = \{\overline{m}_1 \cdot \overline{b}_1, \ldots, \overline{m}_k \cdot \overline{b}_k\}$ is resource base of the system, that is, STS possesses $\overline{m}_1$ objects $\overline{b}_1$, ..., $\overline{m}_k$ objects $\overline{b}_k$. As it is easy to see, order $q = \{m_1 \cdot b_1, \ldots, m_l \cdot b_l\}$ may be completed by this system, if there exists multiset $v \in \overline{V}_{S_q}$ such that

$$v \subseteq \overline{v}, \tag{21}$$

that is, collection of resources, belonging to the STS, is sufficient for order q completion by one of the implementable ways. In this case order completion is possible. Otherwise, that is, if there is no one multiset $v \in \overline{V}$ satisfying (21), then system is not able to complete q.

Example 5. Let KB from Example 2 be STS technological base, while

$$
\begin{aligned}
\overline{v} = \{&6 \cdot \textit{transmission}, 10 \cdot \textit{wheel}, 2 \cdot \textit{fuel-cistern}, 7 \cdot \textit{front-glass},\\
&9 \cdot \textit{back-glass}, 180 \cdot \langle \textit{mnt-car} \rangle, 240 \cdot \langle \textit{mnt-body} \rangle, 600 \cdot \langle \textit{mnt-engine} \rangle,\\
&1000000 \cdot \textit{eur}, 500000 \cdot \textit{usd}\}
\end{aligned}
$$

is its resource base. As may be seen, this resource base is not sufficient for order $q = \{3 \cdot \textit{car}\}$ from Example 11 completion, because condition (21) is not satisfied: there are objects, entering all $v \in \overline{V}_{S_q}$, which do not enter $\overline{v}$ at all (*motor*, *accumulator*, etc.). At the same time multiplicities of some terminal objects are less than it is necessary for order q completion $\left(2 \cdot \textit{fuel-cistern} \in \overline{v} \text{ while } 3 \cdot \textit{fuel-cistern} \in v \in \overline{V}_{S_q}\right)$. ■

After recognition of system's inability to complete order q, there may be two questions:

1. What amount of resources must be acquired by the system to complete the order?

2. What part of order may be completed, given resources, owned by STS?

The answer to the first question is obvious: if $v \in \overline{V}_{S_q}$, and v is not subset of $\overline{v}$, then additional amount of resources, necessary for order completion, is $\overline{v}-v$. Thus variants of necessary resources acquisition are elements of set of terminal multisets

$$\Delta\overline{V}_{S_q} = \left\{\overline{v}-v \middle| v \in \overline{V}_{S_q}\right\}. \tag{22}$$

The answer to the second question concerned reader may find in [1], where the so-called reverse multigrammars are used for this problem solution.

One more area of useful application of UMG/UMMG is **assessment of sociotechnical systems sustainability/vulnerability to various destructive impacts,** which was in details considered in [1]. The main result of this work is as follows.

Let R_q be scheme, corresponding to technological base of the system and order q in the sense (17)–(19); $\overline{v}$ is total resource of this system (resource base, joined with multiset representation of technological base, as it was suggested in [1]), and $\Delta\overline{v}$ is impact, destructing some part of the aforementioned total resource. We shall call STS with technological base R and total resource $\overline{v}$ sustainable to impact $\Delta\overline{v}$ while completing order q, if

$$\left(\exists v \in \overline{V}_{S_q}\right) v \subseteq \overline{v} - \Delta\overline{v}. \tag{23}$$

That is, despite impact there is at least one way of order completion. Otherwise, if there is no one TMS $v \in \overline{V}_{S_q}$, satisfying (23), considered STS is vulnerable to impact $\Delta\overline{v}$.

4. Optimization problems

Another important issue to be discussed here is **profit optimization in production economy** (POPE). We shall consider it not only because of its practical value but also in order to illustrate techniques of UMG/UMMG application to the multigrammatical representation and solution of classical optimization problems.

POPE is formulated as follows [15]. Let there be n products, manufactured by STS, x_i is amount of i-th product, and c_i is its price. Profit, which producing STS would obtain, is

$$C = \sum_{i=1}^{m} c_i \cdot x_i. \tag{24}$$

To produce one unit of i-th product, the system needs respective resources, namely, a_{ij} units of the j-th resource, where $j = 1, ..., n$, and n is total number of different resources, consumed by the system for production. There are $b_1, ..., b_n$ amount of resources available, and the problem is to maximize profit C under restrictions

$$\sum_{i=1}^{m} a_{ij}x_i \le b_j, \tag{25}$$

where $j = 1, ..., n$.

This problem may be represented by unitary multiset metagrammar $S = <q, R, F>$, which scheme R contains one unitary metarule

$$q \to x_1 \cdot u_1, ..., x_m \cdot u_m, \tag{26}$$

where $x_1, ..., x_m$ are variables, and m unitary rules

$$u_i \to ai_1 \cdot e_1, ..., ai_n \cdot e_n, c_i \cdot e, \tag{27}$$

where $i = 1, ..., m$, and a_{ij} is nonzero amount of j-th resource, needed for i-th product, while c_i is its price. Filter F contains n boundary conditions

$$e_j \le b_j, \tag{28}$$

where $j = 1, ..., n$, as well as one optimizing condition

$$e = \max, \tag{29}$$

along with m variable declarations

$$0 \le x_i \le M_i, \tag{30}$$

where $i = 1, ..., m$ and M_i is maximal amount of i-th product, which may be manufactured by the system. As seen, terminal objects $e_1, ..., e_n$ are measurement units of corresponding resources, while terminal object e is price measurement unit. Nonterminal objects $u_1, ..., u_m$ represent products, and UMR (26) along with optimizing condition (29) represents order, while n URs (27) represent STS technological base. STS resource base, as it was introduced higher, is represented by boundary conditions (28).

As may be seen, set of POPE solutions is

$$\overline{V_S} = \{v_1, ..., v_t\}, \tag{31}$$

where

$$\{l_1 \cdot e_1, ..., l_n \cdot e_n, C \cdot e, p_1 \cdot \overline{x}_1, ..., p_m \cdot \overline{x}_m\} \in \overline{V_S} \tag{32}$$

means that maximal profit is C and it is gotten when STS produces p_1 units of the first product, ..., p_m units of the m-th product. In general case

$$|\overline{V_S}| > 1, \tag{33}$$

so there may be $t > 1$ solutions of the specific POPE.

Example 6. Let POPE is

$$2x_1 + 3x_2 \to \max$$

under restrictions

$$3x_1 + 2x_2 \le 10$$

$$5x_1 + 3x_2 \le 18.$$

That means STS is producing two products, which prices are 2 and 3, respectively, and there is resource base, containing 10 units of the first resource and 18 units of the second. To produce one unit of the first product, STS needs 3 units of the first resource and 5 units of the second, while producing of one unit of the second product needs 2 units of the first resource and 3 units of the second resource.

According to (26)–(30), scheme R of the corresponding UMMG $S = <q, R, F>$ includes UMR

$$q \to x_1 \cdot u_1, x_2 \cdot u_2,$$

as well as two URs:

$$u_1 \to 3 \cdot e_1, 5 \cdot e_1, 2 \cdot e,$$
$$u_2 \to 2 \cdot e_1, 3 \cdot e_2, 3 \cdot e.$$

Filter F contains two boundary conditions

$$e_1 \leq 10,$$
$$e_2 \leq 18,$$

one optimizing condition

$$e = \max,$$

as well as two variables declarations:

$$0 \leq x_1 \leq 10,$$
$$0 \leq x_2 \leq 10,$$

where 10 is maximal amount of any product, which may be produced by STS.
As seen,

$$\overline{V}_S = \{\{10 \cdot e_1, 16 \cdot e_2, 10 \cdot \text{e}, 2 \cdot \overline{x}_1, 2 \cdot \overline{x}_2\}\},$$

which means STS would get maximal profit of 10 units, producing 2 units of both products and, spending for that purpose, 10 units of the first resource and 16 units of the second resource. ■

Let us note that classical matrix–vector POPE modeling is limiting set of the considered cases to the simplest two-level structures of the manufactured objects ("object-component"), represented by unitary rules like (27). In practice, all such objects have much more complicated, multilevel heterogeneous hierarchical structure, that is clearly illustrated by the previous Examples 1–3, concerning car manufacturing.

UMMG application provides natural representation of the POPE problem in the most general formulation. Namely, it is sufficient to join to set of URs, describing technological base of the STS, the only UMR like (26). Similarly, to represent resource base of the STS, filter of the created UMMG would contain boundary conditions like (28); it is important that absence of some resource e in the RB must be represented by boundary condition $e = 0$; otherwise any generated TMS, containing multiobject $n \cdot e$, where $n > 0$, may enter one of the solutions, and this contradicts reality. The goal of STS is defined by the optimizing condition like (29), and domains of variables, having place in the aforementioned UMR, are defined by variable declarations like (30). If it is necessary to maximize profit, taking into account expenses for some resources acquisition, it is very convenient to use representation of prices of the acquired resources, as it was illustrated by Example 4, but with negative multiplicities (such techniques are described in [2, 3]), that is, as to URs from Example 4,

$$\begin{aligned} &\textit{transmission} \rightarrow \text{-}100 \cdot \textit{usd}, \\ &\textit{wheel} \rightarrow \text{-}50 \cdot \textit{usd}, \\ &\dots \\ &\textit{accumulator} \rightarrow \text{-}10 \cdot \textit{usd}. \end{aligned}$$

To cut off generated TMS with nonpositive multiplicities of object e (such TMS correspond to unprofitable variants), it is sufficient to join to UMMG filter one more boundary condition $e > 0$. However, the use of negative multiplicities leads to some corrections in UMG/UMMG algorithmics, which would be considered separately.

All the said higher in this section is very close to the Leontief model and other "input–output" models of mathematic economy, developed on the matrix–vector algebra basis [16]. As may be seen, transfer to the UMG/UMMG basis makes such modeling much more flexible and closer to the reality. That is why we consider multigrammatical paradigm as very perspective for the development of various issues in the future digital economy [17, 18], first of all, planning and scheduling in the cyberphysical industry, integrated with deeply robotized logistics [19, 20]. However, application of the described here approach to the core areas of digital economy (Industry 4.0) needs separate publications.

Concerning implementation issues, it would be aptly to say that multisets processing is very promising area for application of non-conventional computing paradigms [21, 22].

Now let us spend some place of this section for **multiset modeling of competitions and works distribution in the concurrent environment**, typical for market economy.

The main tool of the last is the so-called variative unitary multigrammars and multimetagrammars, which schemes include unitary rules (metarules) with the same head and different bodies. UMG/UMMG variativity provides representation of coexistence of various subjects able to complete one and the same order. We assume these subjects are non-antagonistic, that is, they all are ready to execute any part of the total work.

There may be at least three possible approaches to multigrammatical modeling of competitions:

1. "The winner takes it all."

2. Splitting order among various subjects.

3. "The winner coalition takes it all" (combination of two previous).

Let us consider the *first* approach.

Let R be set of unitary rules containing, among others, k URs with one and the same head and different bodies:

$$\begin{aligned} a &\leftarrow n_1^1 \cdot a_1^1, \dots, n_{m_1}^1 \cdot a_{m_1}^1, \\ &\dots \\ a &\leftarrow n_1^k \cdot a_1^k, \dots, n_{m_k}^k \cdot a_{m_k}^k. \end{aligned} \tag{34}$$

where i-th alternative corresponds to i-th subject of considered technological base, able to produce object a, consuming for that purpose

n_1^i objects $a_1^i, \ldots, n_{m_i}^i$ objects $a_{m_i}^i$. To simplify and unify recognition of variant implemented, let us introduce k terminal objects $s_1, \ldots, s_k$, being names of corresponding subjects, and replace set (34) by

$$\begin{gathered} a \leftarrow 1 \cdot s_1, n_1^1 \cdot a_1^1, \ldots, n_{m_1}^1 \cdot a_{m_1}^1, \\ \ldots \\ a \leftarrow 1 \cdot s_k, n_1^k \cdot a_1^k, \ldots, n_{m_k}^k \cdot a_{m_k}^k. \end{gathered} \tag{35}$$

Let $q = \{n \cdot a\}$, and R_q is set of URs, containing UR

$$a_q \rightarrow n \cdot a, \tag{36}$$

k URs (35), and all unitary rules from set R, excluding (35). Consider UMG $S_q = \langle a_q, R_q \rangle$. As seen, $\overline{V}_{S_q}$ is set of terminal multisets, each corresponding to some variant of order q completion. If we establish filter F_q to select one and only one element of $\overline{V}_{S_q}$, transforming UMG S_q to FUMG $S_q = \langle a_q, R_q, F_q \rangle$, this element will be

$$\left\{ n \cdot s_i, m_1^i \cdot \overline{b}_1^i, \ldots, m_{l_i}^i \cdot \overline{b}_{l_i}^i \right\}, \tag{37}$$

where multiobject $n \cdot s_i$ corresponds to n operation cycles of subject s_i during order q completion and every multiobject $m_j^i \cdot \overline{b}_j^i$ corresponds to m_j^i terminal objects $\overline{b}_j^i$, required for these cycles' implementation. In this context, filter F_q may contain boundary conditions, defining required resources limits, as well as optimizing conditions, defining some of terminal object $\overline{b}_j^i$ multiplicities as minimal (e.g., cost, electrical energy, or fuel consumed) or maximal (e.g., some integral parameters of quality of produced objects or given services). If subject s_i becomes the only winner, it takes all order to complete.

Example 7. Let us consider following unitary rules:

$$\begin{aligned} &car \rightarrow 1 \cdot first,\ 30 \cdot \langle mnt\text{-}car \rangle, 2800 \cdot usd, 1 \cdot accessories - set, \\ &car \rightarrow 1 \cdot \text{second},\ 40 \cdot \langle mnt\text{-}car \rangle, 2700 \cdot usd, 1 \cdot accessories - set, \\ &car \rightarrow 1 \cdot third,\ 45 \cdot \langle mnt\text{-}car \rangle, 2500 \cdot usd, 1 \cdot accessories - set. \end{aligned}$$

These URs being joined with URs, detailing nonterminal object *accessories set* from R, describe competition of three car manufacturers (first, second, and third), assembling cars from one and the same accessories but differing by the time spent for this operation and its cost. If we consider FUMG $S_q = \langle a_q, R, F \rangle$, where $q = \{3 \cdot car\}$ and $F = \{usd = \min\}$, then

$$\overline{V}_{S_q} = \{\{1 \cdot third, X \cdot usd, 135 \cdot \langle mnt \cdot car \rangle, \ldots\}\},$$

which corresponds to the choice of the third manufacturer. If $F = \{usd = \min, \langle mnt\text{-}car \rangle = \min\}$, then

$$\overline{V}_{S_q} = \{\varnothing\},$$

because no one of the possible order executors is optimal by time and cost simultaneously. ■

As it is well known from practice, approach, described higher, may be not rational from various points of view, especially, when capabilities of no one of the competitors (subjects $s_1, ..., s_k$) are not sufficient for the whole order completion. In this case, more rational may be the *second* approach when order is splitted between non-antagonistic (cooperating) competitors in such a way that the total amount of objects produced is distributed among subjects $s_1, ..., s_k$. This techniques may be modeled by unitary multimetagrammar S_q, which scheme R_q includes unitary metarule

$$a_q \rightarrow \gamma_1 \cdot b_1, ..., \gamma_k \cdot b_k, \tag{38}$$

and unitary rules

$$\begin{gathered} b_1 \rightarrow 1 \cdot a, n_1^1 \cdot a_1^1, ..., n_{l_1}^1 \cdot a_{l_1}^1, \\ ... \\ b_k \rightarrow 1 \cdot a, n_1^k \cdot a_1^k, ..., n_{l_k}^k \cdot a_{l_k}^k, \end{gathered} \tag{39}$$

as well as all URs, having place in the scheme, constructed higher by application of the first approach, excluding (34). Filter F_q contains boundary condition

$$a = n, \tag{40}$$

which is directly induced by order $q = \{n \cdot a\}$ and boundary conditions, defining domains of variables $\gamma_1, ..., \gamma_k$:

$$0 \leq \gamma_i \leq n. \tag{41}$$

As seen, terminal multisets, generated by UMMG $S = \langle a_q, R_q, F_q \rangle$, have form

$$\left\{n \cdot a, n_1 \cdot \overline{\gamma}_1, ..., n_k \cdot \overline{\gamma}_k, m_1^i \cdot \overline{b}_1^i, ..., m_{l_i}^i \cdot \overline{b}_{l_i}^i\right\}, \tag{42}$$

where, according to (38)–(40),

$$\sum_{i=1}^{k} n_i = n, \tag{43}$$

and thus values $n_1, ..., n_k$ are parts of order $q = \{n \cdot a\}$, distributed among subjects $s_1, ..., s_k$, respectively: s_1 will produce n_1 objects a, $s_2 - n_2$ objects a, up to s_k, which will produce n_k objects a.

Example 8. Let us transform set R from Example 7 to the following:

order $\rightarrow \gamma_1 \cdot$ *first*, $\gamma_2 \cdot$ second, $\gamma_3 \cdot$ *third*,

first $\rightarrow 1 \cdot$ *car*, 2800 $\cdot$ *usd*, 2800 $\cdot$ *usd-1*, 1 $\cdot$ *accessories-set*,

second $\rightarrow 1 \cdot$ *car*, 2500 $\cdot$ *usd*, 2500 $\cdot$ *usd-2*, 1 $\cdot$ *accessories-set*,

third $\rightarrow 1 \cdot$ *car*, 2200 $\cdot$ *usd*, 2200 $\cdot$ *usd-3*, 1 $\cdot$ *accessories-set*.

If order $q = \{10 \cdot car\}$, then $F_q = \{car = 10, 0 \leq \gamma_1 \leq 10, 0 \leq \gamma_2 \leq 10, 0 \leq \gamma_3 \leq 10\} \cup F'_q$, where F'_q may contain boundary and optimizing conditions, selecting terminal multisets, for example, $F'_q = \{usd = \min, usd\text{-}1 \geq 2800, usd\text{-}2 \geq 5000, usd\text{-}3 \geq 6600\}$. According to such F_q, set of terminal multisets, generated by UMMG $S_q = \langle a_q, R_q, F_q \rangle$, may contain element of the form $\{10 \cdot car, 25600 \cdot usd, 14000 \cdot usd\text{-}1, 5000 \cdot usd\text{-}2, 6600 \cdot usd\text{-}3, \ 5 \cdot \gamma_1, 2 \cdot \gamma_2, 3 \cdot \gamma_3, ...\}$, which corresponds to splitting order q in such a way that five cars would be assembled by the first manufacturer, two by the second, and three by the third. ∎

Let us underline once more that time is not additive resource in relation to parallel processes; it is additive only regarding one device (manufacturing unit). Consideration of multisets with time-containing multiobjects is separate direction of the multigrammatical approach and needs special tool, which is called temporal multiset grammars (TMG), announced in [1] . This branch concerns problems, addressed by the classical theory of scheduling [23, 24].

The third possible case of competitions ("the winner coalition takes it all") may be considered by the concerned reader on his (her) own.

5. Conclusion

Presented primary survey of multigrammatical knowledge representation along with brief consideration of its possible applications is, of course, only a background for future development, which most valuable directions may be:

1. MG/UMG/UMMG extension by features, necessary for "single-time-scale" modeling of manufacturing and logistical processes and their optimal control, that is critically needed for the developed digital economy (Industry 4.0)

2. Development of algorithmics for local correction of solutions (generated sets of TMS) while UMG/UMMG local correction in the sense [25], which is necessary for the aforementioned control in hard real-time and highly volatile environment

3. Further development of MG/UMG/UMMG improved algorithmics and its software/hardware implementation in high-parallel general-purpose computing environments

4. Development of specialized high-parallel computing environments, initially oriented to MG/UMG/UMMG algorithmics implementation

5. Development of quantum, neural and molecular algorithmics for MG/UMG/UMMG toolkit implementation in corresponding computer environments

6. MG/UMG/UMMG pragmatics expansion to new problem areas and convergence with other known knowledge/data engineering paradigms (first of all, multiagent systems [15, 26, 27])

Some of the listed directions are already developed by the author and his colleagues; some are waiting their time, being targeted to the creation of unified framework for the intellectual (knowledge-based) digital economy. This way is leading us to the Big Knowledge paradigm being generalization of the Big Data one, which is already everyday reality. The author will be glad, if this paper will be of any interest for some scholars working in the related areas.

Acknowledgements

The author is grateful to Prof. Fred Roberts for useful discussions and support, and to Prof. Jeffrey Ullman, whose useful remarks on the primary version of this work contributed to its essential upgrade. A significant incentive for the development of the proposed approach was its positive assessment by Prof. Noam Chomsky, which early works on syntactic structures formed a conceptual background of the described mathematical toolkit.

Author details

Igor Sheremet
Financial University under the Government of Russian Federation, Moscow, Russia

*Address all correspondence to: sheremet@rfbr.ru

References

[1] Sheremet I. Multiset analysis of consequences of natural disasters impacts on large-scale industrial systems. Data Science Journal. **17**(4): 1-17. DOI: 10.5334/dsj-2018-004

[2] Sheremet IA. Recursive Multisets and Their Applications. Moscow: Nauka; 2010. p. 293. (In Russian)

[3] Sheremet IA. Recursive Multisets and Their Applications. Berlin: NG Verlag; 2011. p. 249

[4] Lasdon SL. Optimization Theory for Large Systems. NY: Dover Publications; 2013. p. 560

[5] Hemmecke R, Koppe M, Lee J, Weismantel R. Nonlinear Integer Programming. In: 50 Years of Integer Programming 1958–2008: The Early Years and State-of-the-Art Surveys. NY: Springer-Verlag; 2009. pp. 1-57. DOI: 10.1007/978-3-540-68279-0-15

[6] Ershov AP. On the partial computation principle. Information Processing Letters. 1977;**2**(2):38-41

[7] Bjorner D, Ershov AP, Jones ND, editors. Partial Evaluation and Mixed Computation. North Holland: Amsterdam; 1988. p. 625

[8] Itkin VE. An algebra of mixed computation. Theoretical Computer Science. 1991;**90**(1):81-93

[9] Lloyd JW, Shepherdson JC. Partial evaluation in logic programming. Journal of Logic Programing. 1991;**11** (3–4):217-242. DOI: 10.1016/0743-1066 (91)90027–M

[10] Hansen E. Global optimization using interval analysis—The one-dimensional case. Journal of Optimization Theory and Applications. 1979;**29**:331-334

[11] Hansen E. Global Optimization Using Interval Analysis. NY: Marcel Dekker; 1992. p. 284

[12] Hansen E, Walster GW. Global Optimization Using Interval Analysis. NY: Marcel Dekker; 2004. p. 530

[13] Fiedler M, Nedoma J, Ramik J, Rohn J, Zimmerman K. Linear Optimization Problems with Inexact Data. NY: Springer; 2006. p. 227

[14] Sheremet IA. Augmented Post Systems: The Mathematical Framework for Knowledge and Data Engineering in Network-Centric Environment. Berlin: EANS; 2013. p. 395

[15] Shoham Y, Leyton-Brown K. Multiagent Systems. Algorithmic, Game-Theoretic, and Logical Foundations. Cambridge, UK: Cambridge University Press; 2009. p. 532

[16] Bjerkholt O, Kuzz HD. Introduction: The history of input-output analysis, Leontief's path and alternative tracks. Economic Systems Research. 2006; **18**(4):331-333. DOI: 10.1080/ 09535310601030850

[17] Schwab K. The Fourth Industrial Revolution. What It Means and How to Respond. Foreign Affairs. December 12, 2015. Available from: https://foreignaffairs.com/articles/2015-12-12/fourth-industrial-revolution

[18] Baller S, Dutta S, Lanvin B, editors. The Global Information Technology Report 2016. Innovating in the Digital Economy. Geneve: WEF and INSEAD; 2016. p. 62

[19] Colombo AW, Bangemann T, Karnouskos T, Delsing J, Stluka P, Harrison R, et al. Industrial Cloud-Based Cyber-Physical Systems:

The IMC-AESOP Approach. NY: Springer Verlag; 2014. p. 245

[20] Lee J, Bagheri B, Hung-An K. A cyber-physical systems architecture for Industry 4.0-based manufacturing systems. Manufacturing Letters. 2015;**3**: 18-23. DOI: 10.1016/j.mfglet.2014.12.001

[21] Montanaro A. Quantum algorithms: An overview. npj Quantum Information. 2015;**2**:15023. DOI: 10.1038/npjqi.2015.23

[22] Farhi E, Goldstone J, Gutmann S. A quantum approximate optimization algorithm applied to a bonded occurrence constraint problem. In: Quantum Physics. Report MIT-CTP/4628. NY: Cornell University, 2015. arXiv: 1412.6062

[23] Conway RW, Maxwell WL, Miller LW. Theory of Scheduling. Mineola, NY: Dover Publications; 2003. p. 304

[24] Leung JY-T, editor. Handbook of Scheduling: Algorithms, Models, and Performance Analysis. NY: Chapman & Hall/CRC; 2004. p. 1224

[25] Sheremet IA. Intelligent Software Environments for Computerized Information Processing Systems. Moscow: Nauka; 1994. p. 544. (In Russian)

[26] Wooldridge M. An Introduction to Multi-Agent Systems. Chichester, England: John Wiley & Sons; 2009. p. 460

[27] Salamon T. Design of Agent-Based Models. Repin-Zivolin: Brukner Publishing; 2011. p. 220